Cambridge Primary
Science
Teacher's Guide 5
Second Edition

Series editors:
Judith Amery
Rosemary Feasey

with Boost Subscription

To get full access to all the Teacher's Guide resources this handbook must be used alongside your online Boost subscription.

HODDER EDUCATION
AN HACHETTE UK COMPANY

Cambridge International copyright material in this publication is reproduced under licence and remains the intellectual property of Cambridge Assessment International Education.

Registered Cambridge International Schools benefit from high-quality programmes, assessments and a wide range of support so that teachers can effectively deliver Cambridge Primary. Visit www.cambridgeinternational.org/primary to find out more.

The knowledge tests and answers have been written by the authors. These may not fully reflect the approach of Cambridge Assessment International Education.

Third-party websites and resources referred to in this publication have not been endorsed by Cambridge Assessment International Education.

Acknowledgements
The Publishers would like to thank the following for permission to reproduce copyright material. Every effort has been made to trace or contact all copyright holders, but if any have been inadvertently overlooked, the Publishers will be pleased to make the necessary arrangements at the first opportunity.

Video acknowledgments
p. 40 © Kmotion/Shutterstock.com; **p. 44** © Flower Time Lapse/Shutterstock.com; **p. 45** © Wolfgang Amri/Shutterstock.com; **p. 84** © Rebus_Productions/Shutterstock

Photo acknowledgements
p. 4 *cc* © Dimazel/Adobe Stock Photo; **p. 10** *br* © Elena Elisseeva/123rf; **p. 6** *tc* © Luchschen F/ Adobe Stock Photo; *cc* © New Africa/Adobe Stock Photo; *bc* © Sven Pfister/Adobe Stock Photo; *br* © Cathleen Howland/Adobe Stock Photo.

t = top, *b* = bottom, *l* = left, *r* = right, *c* = centre

Hachette UK's policy is to use papers that are natural, renewable and recyclable products and made from wood grown in well-managed forests and other controlled sources. The logging and manufacturing processes are expected to conform to the environmental regulations of the country of origin.

Orders: please contact Hachette UK Distribution, Hely Hutchinson Centre, Milton Road, Didcot, Oxfordshire, OX11 7HH. Telephone: +44 (0)1235 827827. Email education@hachette.co.uk Lines are open from 9 a.m. to 5 p.m., Monday to Friday. You can also order through our website: www.hoddereducation.com

© Rosemary Feasey, Deborah Herridge, Helen Lewis, Tara Lievesley, Andrea Mapplebeck, Hellen Ward 2021

First published in 2017

This edition published in 2021 by
Hodder Education,
An Hachette UK Company
Carmelite House
50 Victoria Embankment
London EC4Y 0DZ

www.hoddereducation.com

Impression number 10 9 8 7 6 5 4 3 2 1
Year   2025 2024 2023 2022 2021

Illustrations by James Hearne, Natalie and Tamsin Hinrichsen, Stéphan Theron

Typeset in FS Albert 11/13 by IO Publishing CC

Printed in the United Kingdom

A catalogue record for this title is available from the British Library.
ISBN 9781398300880

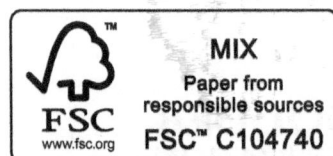

MIX
Paper from responsible sources
FSC™ C104740
FSC
www.fsc.org

Contents

How to use the *Learner's Book*

Structure of the *Learner's Book*

Sections

The *Learner's Book* has four sections that mirror the content covered in the *Cambridge Primary Science* curriculum framework:

Biology **Chemistry** **Physics** **Earth and space**

Units

Within each section, the content is further divided into units. The features used in the units are explained below.

Knowledge tests

A knowledge test for the end of each section is available as part of the online resources at boost-learning.com. This can be used to check learners' mastery of the content covered in all units in the section.

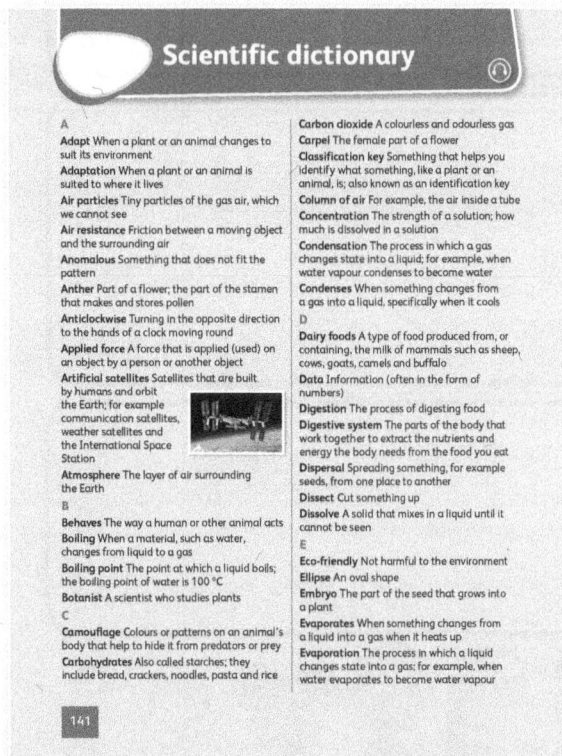

Scientific dictionary

Located at the back of the *Learner's Book*, this dictionary provides simple definitions for the scientific words that learners encounter during this stage.

Scientific dictionary

A

Adapt When a plant or an animal changes to suit its environment

Adaptation When a plant or an animal is suited to where it lives

Air particles Tiny particles of the gas air, which we cannot see

Air resistance Friction between a moving object and the surrounding air

Anomalous Something that does not fit the pattern

Anther Part of a flower; the part of the stamen that makes and stores pollen

Anticlockwise Turning in the opposite direction to the hands of a clock moving round

Applied force A force that is applied (used) on an object by a person or another object

Artificial satellites Satellites that are built by humans and orbit the Earth; for example communication satellites, weather satellites and the International Space Station

Atmosphere The layer of air surrounding the Earth

B

Behaves The way a human or other animal acts

Boiling When a material, such as water, changes from liquid to a gas

Boiling point The point at which a liquid boils; the boiling point of water is 100 °C

Botanist A scientist who studies plants

C

Camouflage Colours or patterns on an animal's body that help to hide it from predators or prey

Carbohydrates Also called starches; they include bread, crackers, noodles, pasta and rice

Carbon dioxide A colourless and odourless gas

Carpel The female part of a flower

Classification key Something that helps you identify what something, like a plant or an animal, is; also known as an identification key

Column of air For example, the air inside a tube

Concentration The strength of a solution; how much is dissolved in a solution

Condensation The process in which a gas changes state into a liquid; for example, when water vapour condenses to become water

Condenses When something changes from a gas into a liquid, specifically when it cools

D

Dairy foods A type of food produced from, or containing, the milk of mammals such as sheep, cows, goats, camels and buffalo

Data Information (often in the form of numbers)

Digestion The process of digesting food

Digestive system The parts of the body that work together to extract the nutrients and energy the body needs from the food you eat

Dispersal Spreading something, for example seeds, from one place to another

Dissect Cut something up

Dissolve A solid that mixes in a liquid until it cannot be seen

E

Eco-friendly Not harmful to the environment

Ellipse An oval shape

Embryo The part of the seed that grows into a plant

Evaporates When something changes from a liquid into a gas when it heats up

Evaporation The process in which a liquid changes state into a gas; for example, when water evaporates to become water vapour

141

Features in each unit

These are the features used in each unit:

What do you remember about the parts of a flower?

a Working with a partner, write down as many parts of a flower as you can in one minute.

b Share your list with another pair. Which words do they have that you do not?

What do you remember about ...?

Found at the start of each unit, these provide an opportunity for learners to recall what they already know, from either their previous learning or life experience. Allows teachers to check prior knowledge and skills and to plan lessons accordingly.

Activity

Provides carefully sequenced steps to cover the central concepts and skills required at this stage. Divides the content into manageable, logical steps to facilitate teaching and learning. Guidance and suggested answers are provided in this *Teacher's Guide*.

Think like a scientist!

Explores scientific subject knowledge, reminding learners of prior learning and introducing them to new learning.

---

1 You will need...
- eight straws
- ruler
- card
- sticky tape
- scissors

a You are going to make your own pan pipes.

b Cut your straws to these lengths: 4 cm, 6 cm, 8 cm, 10 cm, 14 cm, 16 cm, 18 cm and 20 cm.

c Line up your straws from the shortest to the longest. Place sticky tape across the straws to keep them together.

d On both sides of the straws, place a piece of card. This will make a pipe sandwich.

e Play your pan pipes.

f How can you change the volume of the sound?

g What must you do to play a higher or lower sound?

h Make up a tune by changing the volume and pitch.

i Play your tune to someone else. Explain how you change the sounds. Use these words:

(column of air) (volume) (air) (pitch) (vibrate)

Think like a scientist!

An object falls to the ground because of the force of gravity of the Earth acting on the falling object.

Parachutes are used to reduce the effect of gravity. A parachute slows down an object as it falls, increasing air resistance by using a large canopy.

This force diagram shows the forces of air resistance and gravity acting on a parachute.

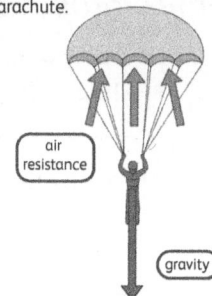

air resistance

gravity

Let's talk

Encourages learners to discuss issues related to the content.

Let's talk

Discuss these questions with a partner:

a Why do you think some flowers are brightly coloured?

b Why do you think some flowers have a strong scent?

Share your ideas with another pair.

Features in each unit

Science in context

Food scientists

Much of the food you eat has been specially designed and made by food scientists.

There are different kinds of food scientists:

Biologists: Biologists play a key role in producing food and drinks, and developing new products. They find new ways of growing crops that will withstand drought conditions due to climate change, develop plants that are resistant to pests, and develop food that has more vitamins and minerals in it.

Food scientist studying samples under a microscope

Biotechnologists: Biotechnologists design systems for producing food. For example, they design systems that turn milk into yoghurt. They also design the machinery used to make different food and drinks.

Chemical engineers: Chemical engineers help to create food additives to make food taste better and look more attractive. They also help design new foods and solve problems. For example, scientists are working on using the waste shells from crabs and prawns to make packaging for food.

Biochemists: Biochemists find out about how living things are made. They help to develop nutritious food by finding out about the different chemicals in food and inventing new chemicals.

Let's talk

Discuss these questions in pairs:

a What kind of food scientist would you like to be?

b What science do you already know that would help you be that kind of food scientist?

c Which of the four food scientists do you think is the most important? What are your reasons for thinking that?

d Find someone in your class who thinks that a different food scientist is the most important. Have a debate. Try to persuade the other person to change their mind. What kind of persuasive language will you use? Try some of these phrases:

Have you considered ...?   In my opinion ...   because ...

I agree with you, but did you know ...   For these reasons ...

Science in context

Shows learners how everyone uses science in daily life, and how some people use it professionally. Content and activities found here assist learners to meet the learning objectives in the *Science in Context* section of the curriculum framework.

Challenge yourself!

Make a magnet obstacle course on your desk, so that the magnet has to work from underneath your desk to move a magnetic object around the obstacles.

Challenge yourself!

Consolidates concepts and extends learners by providing additional activities to do in class or at home.

What can you do?

Found at the end of every unit, is a list of the learning objectives that were covered. The learner-friendly wording assists both learners and teachers to determine whether the learning objectives have been fully mastered.

What can you do?

You have learnt about plants. You can:

✔ identify and name the parts of a flower.

✔ describe the functions of the petals, anthers, stigma and ovary.

✔ say whether all plants produce flowers.

✔ name some plants that do not produce flowers.

Work safely!

Provides advice on how to stay safe.

Work safely!

Only an adult should boil the water and sugar. Stand back while you are observing.

Did you know?

Presents interesting facts and information to encourage learners to be curious and excited about the world of science.

Did you know?

One third of all the food we eat relies on pollinators for reproduction!

Features in each unit

Scientific words

Contains any new scientific vocabulary used on the page. The words are also highlighted in bold text and are defined in the *Scientific dictionary* at the end of the *Learner's Book*.

> **Scientific words**
> stamen
> anther
> filament

Progression icon

Indicates that learners need to build on knowledge or skills learnt in previous stages.

TWS icon

Indicates activities that address Thinking and Working Scientifically (TWS) learning objectives in the curriculum framework.

Cross-curricular links icon

Highlights opportunities for cross-curricular activities. Suggested activities are provided in the *Teacher's Guide* with an explanation of the links to other subjects or Global Perspectives® Challenges.

Model icon

Shows learners that they are using a mental or physical model of something in the real world.

Audio links icon

Indicates content is available as audio. All audio is available to download for free from www.hoddereducation.com/cambridgeextras.

There are additional online resources at boost-learning.com.

These Stage 4–6 characters are used across the series, so teachers and learners will become familiar with them all.

We... all... like... talking... directly... to... learners!

 Elok
 Pia
 David
 Sanchia
 Guss
 Maris
 Jin

Introduction

About the series

Cambridge Primary Science is a series consisting of a *Learner's Book*, *Workbook* and *Teacher's Guide* for each stage of the Cambridge Primary Science curriculum framework.

The books are written by experienced primary practitioners to reflect the science mastery approach covering the Cambridge Primary Science curriculum framework. The content of each of the components is outlined below.

Learner's Book

The structure and content of the *Learner's Book* are based on the Cambridge Primary Science curriculum framework for each stage. There are four sections in each *Learner's Book* covering *Biology*, *Chemistry*, *Physics* and *Earth and space*, with a Knowledge test for each chapter available at boost-learning.com. Each section is divided into units.

Units contain:

- a prompt that asks, *What do you remember about ...?* to encourage learners to recall prior learning and experience
- key *Scientific words*
- key information about concepts in *Think like a scientist!* and *Did you know?*
- activities to build on and develop learners' knowledge, skills and understanding
- activities (with an icon) to develop learners' enquiry skills in *Thinking and Working Scientifically*
- icons to indicate progression from previous stages, models and cross-curricular links
- question prompts to encourage independent thinking about the concept
- *Let's talk* activities to encourage learners to talk about their ideas
- investigations to assess learners' ideas about the concept, with *Work safely!* tips
- *Challenge yourself!* activities to offer practice and extend learners' knowledge, skills and understanding of the concept
- formative assessment activities and a *What can you do?* checklist at the end of each unit
- a knowledge test is available as part of the Boost online materials to be used at the end of the *Biology*, *Chemistry*, *Physics* and *Earth and space* sections to assess learners' knowledge.

Science in Context

- New to this series is *Science in Context* which is designed to develop learners' understanding of how:
  - » scientific knowledge has changed across the years
  - » they can use science to explain how everyday objects work
  - » everyone (including themselves) uses science in their everyday lives
  - » some people use science in their work
  - » science contributes to the way humans can affect the world.

Each unit has one or more pages dedicated to developing the ideas linked to *Science in Context*. Teachers can further support this by:

- taking learners on field visits
- inviting people who use science to share their work with learners
- using local contexts to further develop learners' understanding of science.

Workbook

The *Workbook* can be used for homework or extension activities after completion of the relevant pages in the *Learner's Book*. The *Workbook* builds on what has taken place during the lesson, demonstrating this understanding through:

- activities linked to the learning objectives in the *Learner's Book*
- a self-check page for learners at the end of each unit.

Teacher's Guide

The *Teacher's Guide* supports the teacher to manage and develop the activities in the *Learner's Book* and *Workbook*, and reinforces the learning through:

- a learning objectives overview table for each unit. For Stage 5, most units include an overview of prior learning and experience from the *Cambridge Primary Science Stages 1–4* material
- a list of learning objectives for each topic in the *Learner's Book*
- links to the online resources in Boost (boost-learning.com) that support the topic
- information about each topic – *Background information*
- activities and ideas to introduce the topic – *Starter activity suggestions*
- notes and answers to match the *Learner's Book* – *Activity notes and answers*
- tips on using technology and internet resources – *ICT links*
- supplementary, remedial and extension activities – *Further activities*
- suggestions on how to determine mastery of each learning objective – *Success criteria*
- ways of formatively assessing learners – *Assessment ideas*
- safety advice – *Work safely*!
- answers for the *Workbook*, *Worksheets* and *Slides*

The *Teacher's Guide* also includes tips and advice for teaching Science to learners whose first language is not English.

Icons
- Learner's Book
- Workbook
- Worksheet
- Online resource
- Audio
- TWS activity
- Progression
- Model
- Cross-curricular link

Online resources in Boost

The online resources in Boost (boost-learning.com) further support the *Teacher's Guide* by providing:
- worksheets
- flashcards
- videos
- audio recordings of key words
- visuals for display on a whiteboard
- interactive activities for learners
- knowledge tests
- English Second Language (ESL) support resources for Science:
  » ESL Worksheets for Science
  » a bilingual picture dictionary for Science (*My Science Dictionary*).

The science mastery approach

Adopting the science mastery approach, each unit follows a progressive format to ensure full coverage of the learning objectives. Fully integrated scientific enquiry learning objectives in each unit provide learners with plenty of practice to master these curriculum framework requirements. Learners may complete the units in the *Learner's Book* in any order.

Mastery learning is rooted in the belief that all learners can succeed if given the right input, support and practice. The mastery approach is a teaching strategy that aims to ensure that learners reach a prescribed level of understanding, being secure in their knowledge of a science concept or competent in a skill, before moving on to the next element of learning. The Cambridge Primary Science curriculum framework is a comprehensive mixture of science subject knowledge and practical scientific skills. The activities in the *Learner's Book* are designed to support all learners towards mastery.

Key elements of the mastery approach

Effective assessment for learning

Each unit begins with a series of activities that assess what learners already know and understand about the topic of the unit. These provide teachers with opportunities to assess learners' existing knowledge and skills in a particular curriculum area, and to check that learners are secure in existing ideas and skills before introducing new areas of learning. If learners hold any misconceptions or have an incomplete understanding of an area of science, the teacher can address the knowledge gaps before introducing new learning.

Introducing new ideas and skills

New ideas are then introduced to learners in carefully sequenced steps. If learners have difficulties, the teacher offers different learning opportunities or focused teaching until learners master the skill or concept. Enough time is allocated to this process, rather than moving through learning quickly with only superficial understanding.

Practice and consolidation

Learners are given opportunities to practise the new ideas and skills so that they become confident and competent in them. This enables them to consolidate these ideas and skills by using them in different activities and contexts. Giving learners opportunities to practise their new skills or knowledge in different ways means that they develop scientific fluency. They can then move on to the next idea and skill with confidence.

Synthesising information

In each unit, learners are challenged to build on existing knowledge and understanding, and to combine this with recently introduced ideas, to make secure progress.

Applying and re-applying knowledge, understanding and skills

Learners have frequent opportunities to apply knowledge, understanding and skills in a variety of contexts. Applying knowledge and skills in a new or different context enables teachers, and learners themselves, to assess how secure their knowledge, understanding and skills are. Application is important because it challenges learners to use what they know and to apply their skills in new situations. It also provides teachers with opportunities for assessing progress.

Reflection

Learners are asked to reflect on what they know and can do, individually and with their working partners or groups. Expectations of learning and criteria for successful learning and progress are made explicit to learners throughout. This helps learners to self-assess and to make judgements about what they need to learn next in order to progress. Reflection also offers learners the opportunity to celebrate their progress in scientific learning.

Common features in each unit

To support the mastery approach, each unit has been created to develop learners' mastery through the following common features:

- setting clear learning objectives so that all learners know what they are learning
- sharing explicit success criteria so that learners can judge when they have achieved their learning objectives
- offering learning in small, carefully sequenced steps, breaking learning down into manageable, logical steps

- assessing what learners already know so that they revisit prior understanding, helping both teachers and learners to recognise what learners know and where they are less secure in their understanding
- providing examples of an idea in different ways to help to develop deeper understanding
- using precise and targeted questioning to check and further develop learners' understanding
- challenging learners to make connections between ideas so that they gain deeper understanding
- using *Let's talk* so that learners have to communicate their ideas and ways of working to someone else. Hearing their own and others' ideas provides reinforcement or helps them to develop their own ideas further. It also provides opportunities for teachers to assess learning
- providing learners with opportunities to develop and deepen their learning through *Science in Context* where they learn how science is applied in everyday contexts, how people use science in their jobs, and where they gain an understanding of science through history.

Thinking and Working Scientifically

There are different kinds of scientific enquiry activities that help learners to develop different ideas and ways of working. In each unit, learners experience a range of these types of activities, as explained in the examples in the table. The following examples are from Stage 5.

Activity	What does it mean?	Purpose	Examples
Observing over time	Learners will, for example, use all their senses (where relevant and safe) to observe change over different periods of time, from within a few minutes to an hour, day, week and over a year.	This is particularly important when observing change over longer periods of time to understand, for example, life cycles of animals and plants.	Learners will, for example: • Observe seeds germinating over time. • Observe crystals growing over a week.
Pattern seeking	Learners will, for example, observe patterns in data and numbers, looking for trends and related events in the natural world that cannot easily be controlled.	Patterns (particularly in numbers) can be used to identify a trend or relationships between one or more things.	Learners will, for example: • Look for patterns in the relationship between the area of a parachute and the time taken to fall to the ground.
Identify and classify (grouping)	**Identify:** giving a scientific name to something, such as core, mantle, crust. **Classify:** sorting according to a scientific grouping, such as vertebrate groups, type of material. It usually helps to order a group of objects based on similarities rather than differences. **Group:** sorting according to similar observable features or behaviours, such as size, shape, number of legs, different materials, or types of animals.	Classification is the method used by scientists to order living organisms and materials.	Learners will, for example: • Identify and classify substances as solids, liquids or gases. • Identify and classify flowering and non-flowering plants. • Identify and classify predator adaptations.

Activity	What does it mean?	Purpose	Examples
Fair test (controlled investigations)	A fair test answers a scientific question in a systematic way. It seeks to link cause and effect. It examines the effect that changing one variable has on another, while keeping all other conditions the same. Fair tests are only appropriate to use when exploring variables that are continuous and can be changed. Fair tests are not suitable for investigating natural phenomena, like the weather or living things, such as ourselves, as we cannot change variables in a systematic way.	Learners collect data to identify and explain the relationship between two variables.	Learners will, for example: • Investigate how the shape of an object affects its movement through water.
Research (using secondary sources)	This means finding out information using books, watching videos, using the internet, reading leaflets, asking an expert, and so on.	This is an appropriate approach to answering questions that are impossible or unsafe for learners to answer using first-hand experiences. This type of enquiry enables learners to compare and evaluate information from multiple sources and distinguish opinion from fact. It also leads to an understanding that sometimes in science, questions do not have definitive answers.	Learners might use a book or the Internet to find out about: • The different types of pollution. • The history of artificial satellites.

Thinking and working like a scientist

Stage 5 learners are expected to think and work like a scientist. This is explained on pages 6 and 7 of the *Learner's Book*. For learners to be able to think and work like a scientist, they need to know what science is and who a scientist is and what they do. So, the teacher should engage learners in developing their understanding by talking about and showing them pictures, videos of people who use science and even inviting some into the classroom.

Learners are expected to:

- **Ask questions** when they are uncertain or would like more information.
- Think about and try out their ideas of how to **answer their own questions** or ones suggested by the teacher.
- **Predict** or think about what might happen. Where learners have no or limited prior knowledge, this is likely to be a guess.

- **Work safely** with others and on their own. In Stage 5, learners should be able to start working more independently. However, provide support at all times, and particularly for potentially dangerous activities, such as using knives or candles.

- **Observe**, using all of the senses (where appropriate) to find out about the world around them, for example, exploring materials to find out their properties, which include, feeling textures, and observing the environment around them, listening and looking for evidence of animals.

- **Record** what happens. This could be using an electronic tablet and taking a video or photograph, drawing, writing a sentence, or using a table. At Stage 5, learners will collect standard measures and present their data in various forms, including Venn and Carroll diagrams, bar charts, flow charts and dot plots.

- **Describe** what happened (results) and possible reasons why, with a partner or other learners in the class, paying particular attention to using scientific language and their observations of what happened. This is an early version of drawing conclusions. Learners in Stage 5 are expected to find patterns in their observations and results, recognising that a pattern indicates something that can repeat.

Helping learners to retain information

Language

Learners are introduced to scientific language throughout each unit. New terms are highlighted in bold and placed in a *Scientific words* box. Once introduced, the words may be used frequently in the unit, so that learners have opportunities for repetition, to reinforce the word and its meaning. When learners write or talk about specific ideas and ways of working, they are prompted to use specific vocabulary to ensure that they use key words regularly. This reinforces links between language and ideas and ways of working.

- **Spelling:** Learners are expected to learn how to spell key scientific words and use them regularly. There are also activities that engage learners in, for example, word searches, crosswords and identifying jumbled words. These support learners in learning key scientific words.

- **Revisit and reinforce:** A range of strategies are used so that learners regularly revisit ideas and ways of working; understanding is reinforced and becomes embedded.

- **Different contexts:** Across a unit, learners meet concepts and ways of working scientifically in different contexts. This helps learners to appreciate that ideas are used in many ways and places in their lives. This is also important for checking their learning, if they can apply learning to a new context appropriately this provides useful assessment evidence.

- **Dictionary:** Each *Learner's Book* in the series has a dictionary of all the new scientific words used at each stage, to support learners. To help with pronunciation, key scientific words for each unit are also available as audio clips.

How mastery comes across in the classroom

The units are designed so that learners are engaged in practical activities wherever appropriate. These hands-on experiences demand that they use and apply their understanding and skills. In science, learners are expected to develop increasing independence. Teachers should encourage them to become more able to work on their own, with a partner or in a small group.

The pattern of each unit

Each unit follows a general pattern for teaching and consolidating the unit learning objectives, for example:

- Units begin with a *What do you remember about ...?* activity to help learners think back to prior learning and experience. There are also learner-led practical activities to re-introduce the concept/learning objectives from previous learning linked to the topic. The purpose of these activities is to find out what learners already know, for example, with the use of *Let's talk*. Here teachers can assess how much learners already know or have retained about a scientific topic, and if they have the confidence to move on to new learning. If they are not quite ready, offer some quick activities to revise and consolidate, before moving on to the next step in the unit.

- Learners are introduced to new ideas and ways of working scientifically. The teacher's role here is to encourage learners to engage in activities and share their learning with you, a partner, a small group and the rest of the class. Asking relevant questions, listening to learners, observing what they do, and reading what they write, means that the teacher is continually assessing progress and deciding whether to go over a key idea again or to progress to the next idea.

- At all times, the teacher will expect all learners to use the key words from the *Scientific words* boxes in the *Learner's Book*. This way, they will become confident in using scientific vocabulary.

- Many activities ask learners to share their ideas or findings with other groups. This approach challenges learners to make sense of their ideas and communicate effectively, as well as listen to and reflect on what other groups say.

Strategies for differentiation

While the mastery approach intends for all learners to reach the same level of understanding and security of knowledge before moving on, teachers may need to use a different approach for some learners or spend additional practice time with learners who have specific learning challenges.

Differentiation means changing the teaching and learning process so that the different needs of learners can be accommodated and individual learning maximised. It involves giving learners tasks that best fit their abilities, while meeting the same learning criteria as their peers. For example, groups of learners could be given slightly different tasks to complete, they might be given more time to complete a task, or they could work with an adult who can support them. This will allow all learners to achieve the same learning objectives, but they will reach the goal in slightly different ways.

Breaking down ideas

Concepts, for example, the layers of the Earth, are broken down into small steps so that learners are guided through a concept in a way that is manageable for most learners. By using these small steps, and by mastering each small step, we build up to securing learners' understanding of the bigger concept.

Some ideas for specific age groups cannot easily be broken down into small steps because of the type of concept. For example, a complete circuit is needed for a bulb to light. However, learners can be given electrical components to test this idea.

Repetition and reinforcement

This is important for all learners. It specifically helps learners who need to meet an idea more than once or in a different form, to consolidate learning.

Safety advice

- Where appropriate, safety warnings are identified and explained in the *Teacher's Guide*, and in the *Learner's Book* (under the heading *Work safely!*). Teachers are responsible for ensuring that activities are checked to ensure that they are safe. The notes act as a warning to consider specific safety issues, but the teacher must check the equipment and materials used in the classroom to make sure that safe practices are followed at all times. This series is purchased by many different countries, so teachers must make sure that, for example, plants and foods used in science lessons are safe. It is also important to check which learners may have food allergies or intolerances, before purchasing or using foodstuffs.

- It is good practice to encourage learners to think about working carefully and safely. They should make sure that they, and others with whom they are working, are safe. Before starting an activity, ask learners to discuss with their partners or others in the group, what might be a hazard and could be harmful. Then ask how they will work to make sure that they stay safe.

- When using the internet for research, ensure that learners understand how to be safe online before starting the activity.

Scientific equipment needed for Stage 5

This list shows items that teachers will need, in addition to basic classroom resources such as pencils, pens, crayons, rulers, A4 and A3 sheets of paper, card (thin and thick, in different sizes), scissors, glue, sticky tape, and so on.

Unit number	Unit name	Resources
1	Plant parts	card or paper, real flowers, scissors, tweezers, sticky tape, sticky-backed plastic, magnifying lens or microscope, recyclable materials, electronic tablet or video camera
2	The life cycle of a flowering plant	real flowers, tweezers, pieces of card, timers, magnifying lens or microscope, large beans, container, water, sharp knife, calculator (optional), measuring spoons, pots, potting compost or soil, ruler (optional), seeds
3	Adaptation	sticky notes, pen or pencil, chopsticks, tweezers, bowls, sunflower seeds or raisins, stopwatch, clothes pegs, dry macaroni, modelling dough or clay
4	The digestive system	bananas, crackers, plastic bowls, knives, forks, potato masher, water, sealable plastic sandwich bags, orange juice, scissors, one leg cut from a pair of tights, trays, paper or plastic cups with a hole in the bottom, paper or plastic cups, paper towels, dough, piece of heavy cardboard about A4 size
5	States of matter	plastic cups, water, pens, camera, different liquids, paper towels, tea leaves soaked in water, shallow containers, video camera, wet clay, board, liquids (such as fruit juice, cola, cooking oil), mirrors, ice cubes, scales, flour, rice, salt, sand, sugar, small stones, beakers, spoons, jug, solid materials to mix with water (such as sugar, cornflour, salt, soil, flour, coffee grounds, tea leaves), teaspoons, coffee filters or filter papers, funnels, transparent plastic cups, saucers, measuring jug, pencils, string, glass jars, lolly sticks or straws, caster sugar, saucepan, food colouring
6	Forces	card, ping pong balls, straws, bowl of water, collection of waterproof objects, newton meter, thick books, two ramps (both the same), smooth wood, rough carpet, cardboard rolls (from kitchen paper), shoes, different surfaces to test, force meter, plastic bags, hole punch, string, small figures, modelling clay or dough, stopwatch, objects that do not float in water, bucket, water, mini-whiteboards and pens, cylinder of water, plasticine
7	Sound	containers, tuning forks, water, ping pong balls, string or wool, ruler or spatula, drums, drumsticks, bird seed, balloons, balloon pump, plastic cups, pencils, paper clips, small pieces of wet cloth, boxes or plastic containers, elastic bands of different sizes and thicknesses, recyclable materials, jam jars or bottles of the same size, measuring cylinders, water, food dyes of different colours, wooden spoons, metal spoons, straws, card, sticky tape, scissors
8	Magnetism	collection of different objects, magnets, large sheets of paper, collection of objects made from different materials, steel paper clips, iron filings in a container, collection of materials (such as wood, paper, card, fabric), objects made from magnetic material, measuring equipment

Unit number	Unit name	Resources
9	**Planet Earth**	large sheets of paper, coloured pens, bowls, cups, elastic bands, ice cubes, plastic wrap, hot water, blue food colouring, pens, plastic zip lock bags, tape, filter papers, funnels, warm water, jugs, magnifying glass and/or digital microscope, pieces of synthetic fleece fabric
10	**The Earth in space**	wooden skewers, dough, flashlights, chalk, a globe or a beach ball (with an equator drawn around the middle, and the northern and southern hemispheres labelled), large pieces of paper, pens

Approaches to assessment

Learning objectives

An overview of all the learning objectives with their codes is provided at the beginning of each unit in the *Teacher's Guide*. It is good practice to share these learning objectives with learners at the beginning of each lesson in learner-friendly language. This will ensure that they are clear on the focus of each activity and what they are expected to learn. At the end of each lesson, ask learners to reflect on what they have learnt and to check their understanding against the success criteria.

Background information

This section explains the purpose of the learning and gives key knowledge and understanding that is covered in the activities. This also supports teacher assessment of learners.

Assessing learners' prior understanding and misconceptions

The purpose of the starter activities in the *Teacher's Guide* and the first page of activities in the *Learner's Book* is to further revisit previous learning linked to the unit. The activities help the teacher to assess how confident learners are and to check for any misconceptions. These can then be identified and remedied before continuing with new learning in the unit. The activities are also used to remind learners of previous learning that they will use in the new unit. For Stage 5, the teacher is directed to review key learning objectives covered in Stages 3–4 of the *Cambridge Primary Science* series.

Success criteria

Suggestions for success criteria are given which link directly to the learning objectives at the beginning of the unit notes. The success criteria are used to assess the outcome of the learning that has taken place. The success criteria are, in effect, what successful learning will 'look' like once learners have met the learning objectives.

For example, for Stage 5 Unit 2 (*Learner's Book* pages 24–26), the success criteria are as follows:

Success criteria

While completing the activities, assess and record learners.

Learning objectives	Success criteria
5Be.02 Describe how flowering plants are adapted to attract pollinators and promote seed dispersal.	Learners can explain how flowering plants are adapted to promote seed dispersal.
5Bp.02 Know the stages in the life cycle of a flowering plant.	Learners can explain that seed dispersal is part of the life cycle of a flowering plant.
5Bp.03 Describe how flowering plants reproduce by pollination, fruit and seed production, and seed dispersal.	Learners can describe how plants disperse seeds and explain why.
5TWSp.03 Make predictions, referring to relevant scientific knowledge and understanding within familiar and unfamiliar contexts.	Learners can make predictions and suggest how accurate they were.
5TWSp.04 Plan fair test investigations, identifying the independent, dependent and control variables.	Learners can plan and carry out a fair test on seed dispersal.
5TWSc.01 Sort, group and classify objects, materials and living things through testing, observation and using secondary information.	Learners can sort, group and classify seeds according to how they disperse.
5TWSc.03 Choose equipment to carry out an investigation and use it appropriately.	Learners choose their own equipment and use it appropriately when carrying out an activity.
5TWSc.04 Decide when observations and measurements need to be repeated to give more reliable data.	Learners repeat readings and can explain why.
5TWSa.01 Describe the accuracy of predictions, based on results.	Learners can compare their predictions with results and comment on the accuracy.

These learning objectives are reproduced from the Cambridge Primary Science curriculum framework (0097) from 2020. This Cambridge International copyright material is reproduced under licence and remains the intellectual property of Cambridge Assessment International Education.

Formative assessment

Formative assessment is a form of ongoing assessment that occurs in every lesson. It informs the teacher and the learner of the progress that they are making, linked to the success criteria.

Formative assessment is important because it means that teachers and learners are continually reflecting on how the learning is moving forward. Where necessary, teachers can work with learners during the lesson, to support any issues in learning that emerge.

Formative assessment should be used to inform the next steps in learning, and may influence changes in planning and therefore the next lessons. Formative assessment is a cycle: finding out what learners know, moving learning forward, finding out how that learning has changed (what they know now) and planning the next steps. Where you find that learners are still unsure, stop and take time to revisit an idea or skill, and change the activity or context. Move on to new learning when learning is secure. Assessment is about you (and learners) continually reflecting on learning, and ensuring that teaching is in line with learning.

It is important because it means that teachers and learners are continually reflecting on how the learning is moving forward. Where necessary, teachers can work with learners during the lesson, to support any issues in learning that emerge.

Introduction

Teachers and learners can assess learning easily, in many ways. These are built into units, for example:

- **Let's talk** These are used regularly throughout each unit to encourage learners to talk about their learning in pairs or groups. In this way, they can articulate their ideas and listen to each other. Where appropriate, they can adjust what they are thinking and saying. The teacher's role is to move around the classroom, listening to learners talking to one another, to identify how learning is taking place. Teachers can provide support where ideas may need modelling (demonstrating with an example), or offer new challenges to those learners who are secure in their thinking and ways of working.

- **Application activities** These activities require learners to apply their learning in different contexts or solve a problem. These are important because teachers can better assess whether learning is secure by checking if learners can apply it to a different or new situation.

Formative assessment is placed at the end of each unit in the *Learner's Book* to assess at a key point in time, what learners know, understand and can do. There are *What can you do?* checklists in the *Learner's Book*, and *Self-check* pages in the *Workbook*, which form part of the formative assessment process. At the end of each section of the *Learner's Book*, there is a Knowledge test (available at boost-learning.com) that can also be used for formative assessment. The information gained from formative assessments should be used to inform future planning in order to close any gaps in learners' understanding and skills. Remember that assessment is ongoing. It is built into all units and should not be viewed as something separate, or only to be done when a unit is finished.

Judith Amery and Rosemary Feasey (Series editors)

Unit 1   Plant parts

Review of prior learning

Learning objectives from Stages 1–4	LB pages	WB pages	TG pages
3Bs.01 Describe the function of the major parts of flowering plants (limited to roots, leaves, stems and flowers).	8		20–22
3Bp.02 Know that life processes common to plants and animals include nutrition, growth, movement and reproduction.	8		20–22
3Bp.03 Know that plants need appropriate conditions, including temperature, light and water, to be healthy.	8		20–22

Learning objectives overview

Biology	Online resources	LB pages	WB pages	TG pages
Structure and function	Flashcards/Audio			
5Bs.01 Know that not all plants produce flowers.	Unit 1 Slides 6–8	14–16	8	27–31
5Bs.02 Identify the parts of a flower (limited to petals, sepals, anthers, filaments, stamens, stigma, style, carpel, and ovary).	Worksheet 2 Unit 1 Slides 4–5	11, 12–13, 14–16	4–5, 6–7	23–27, 27–31
5Bs.03 Describe the functions of the parts of a flower (limited to petals, anthers, stigma and ovary).		11, 12–13, 14–16	4–5	22, 23–27, 27–31

Thinking and Working Scientifically	LB pages	WB pages	TG pages
Models and representations			
5TWSm.01 Know that a model presents an object, process or idea in a way that shows some of the important features.	14, Activity 1		27–31
5TWSm.02 Use models, including diagrams, to represent and describe scientific phenomena and ideas.	14, Activity 1		27–31
Carrying out scientific enquiry			
5TWSc.02 Complete a key based on easily observed differences.	16, Activity 1–2		27–31
5TWSc.08 Collect and record observations and/or measurements in tables and diagrams appropriate to the type of scientific enquiry.	10, Activity 1		22–24

Science in Context	LB pages	WB pages	TG pages
5SIC.04 Identify people who use science, including professionally, in their area and describe how they use science.	9	6	21–22

These learning objectives are reproduced from the Cambridge Primary Science curriculum framework (0097) from 2020. This Cambridge International copyright material is reproduced under licence and remains the intellectual property of Cambridge Assessment International Education.

Cross-curricular links	LB pages	WB pages	TG pages
English	14, Activity 3		28
Global Perspectives® Challenge: Will a robot do your job?	9, Activity 2		21

Focus on working like a botanist

Learner's Book
pages 8–9

Worksheet 1

Unit 1 Slides 1–4
Unit 1 Flashcards

Unit 1 Audio

Learning objectives

Revision of:
- **3Bs.01** *Describe the function of the major parts of flowering plants (limited to roots, leaves, stems and flowers).*
- **3Bp.02** *Know that life processes common to plants and animals include nutrition, growth, movement and reproduction.*
- **3Bp.03** *Know that plants need appropriate conditions, including temperature, light and water, to be healthy.*
- **5SIC.04** *Identify people who use science, including professionally, in their area and describe how they use science.*

Background information

Page 8 of the *Learner's Book* focuses on eliciting what learners already know about plants from previous stages. Use this as an opportunity for formative assessment to find out how secure they are in their knowledge and understanding. Learners work in groups to share what they know and are given questions to prompt them to remember information about plant parts and their function, what plants need to survive, their habitats and other ideas that they might have developed from, for example, gardening at home with family, visits to local parks and watching television programmes.

Learners share their work with one another. The use of challenging learners to choose 3 new words from another group, 2 new facts and to ask 1 question of the other group is to ensure that learners engage with ideas from peers as well as broaden their own knowledge.

The *Science in context* activity on page 9 shares information about the role of a botanist. Developing learners' appreciation of different scientists helps to broaden their understanding of the way people use science-related skills and qualifications for jobs in the wider world.

Starter activity suggestions

- To help prompt learners' memories, display a range of plants including seeds, seedlings and flowers for each group to observe and think about.
- Take learners outside into the school grounds or locality to observe plants, making notes and taking photographs or video clips of things of interest to share and discuss back in the classroom.
- Use Unit 1 Slide 2 (boost-learning.com) to support an explanation about the mind-mapping activity.
- Use Worksheet 1 (boost-learning.com) to revise the functions of parts of a plant.

Unit 1 Slide 2 answers

Mind mapping – sharing what you know

a To help remind learners of what they already know and also to share knowledge.

b To focus on the correct scientific vocabulary reminding them of words they might need to use in this unit.

c To remind them of things they have not remembered as well as learn new facts.

d Help to prompt them to think more deeply about what they know.

Unit 1 Slide 3 answers

Is it a plant?

a All except the lizard.

b They have green leaves, a stem, roots and some have flowers. They need light, air and water to live.

Unit 1 Slide 4 answers

Parts of a plant

a 1 – flower   2 – stem   3 – leaf   4 – fruit   5 – trunk   6 – roots

b Flowers attract insects for pollination.

The stem holds up the leaves, flowers and fruits, keeps the leaves in the light and transport water and nutrients to parts of the plant.

The function of the leaves is to make food for the plant.

The functions of the roots are to anchor the plant in the ground and to take up water and nutrients from the soil.

Activity notes and answers

Page 8 Mind mapping plants
Activity 1

a Reluctant writers might feel more motivated if they wrote on sticky notes and put them on the mind map. Learners could write in one colour and add in more information in other colours as they progress through the unit.

b Accept learners' responses. Encourage learners to discuss ideas prior to writing them down and visit groups to ask questions to prompt memory and ask for clarification.

Activity 2

Give learners time to engage with the work of another group, encourage them to discuss what the other group has written and remind learners that they can learn from others as well as help others with new ideas.

Activity 3

Questions may be quite diverse, they could either use lesson time to research the question or the task could be a home/school activity.

Page 9 Science in context: Working like a botanist
Activity 1

You could give learners question stems such as *what*, *where*, *why*, *who*, *when* and *what if* to prompt their thinking about what else they want to find out about botanists.

Activity 2

a Accept reasonable responses and support learners who might struggle by giving them some alternatives to think about, for example how to stop plant diseases or find cures for diseases using plants. Ask if they would like to work in a laboratory, outdoors or go on a plant exploration to remote places in the world. Learners might suggest, for example, helping to create plants that withstand drought, or stop plagues of locusts eating them.

b Check learners' lists.

c Learners might suggest identifying plants in their area, planting plants that encourage insects, and making the area look more pleasant.

> **Global Perspectives® Challenge**
> **What are the benefits of work?**
>
> **Activity 2** Learners carry out additional research to find out more about a career as a botanist. Ask learners to list the advantages of being a botanist, for example working outdoors, and so on.

Further activities

- Contact your local university to find out if a student botanist or lecturer would visit and talk about their work with your class. You can send their questions by email, or have an online question and answer session.
- Name each group in the class after a famous botanist. The group could research information about the person they are named after.

ICT links

Learners photograph or video plants in the school grounds or locality.

Assessment ideas

The mind map on page 8 provides an opportunity to carry out a formative assessment to find out what learners remember and understand from previous stages, and what personal knowledge gained from out of school experiences they bring to this topic.

Success criteria

While completing the activities, assess and record learners.

Learning objectives	Success criteria
3Bs.01 Describe the function of the major parts of flowering plants (limited to roots, leaves, stems and flowers).	Learners can name parts of a plant and describe their functions.
3Bp.02 Know that life processes common to plants and animals include nutrition, growth, movement and reproduction.	Learners can describe what plants need to grow and how they know they are living.
3Bp.03 Know that plants need appropriate conditions, including temperature, light and water, to be healthy.	Learners can describe what conditions a plant needs to grow and be healthy.
5SIC.04 Identify people who use science, including professionally, in their area and describe how they use science.	Learners can describe what botanists do and how they use their science.

Focus on flowering plants

Learner's Book pages 10–11

Worksheet 2

Unit 1 Slide 5
Visual 1

Learning objectives

- **5Bs.02** Identify the parts of a flower (limited to petals, sepals, anthers, filaments, stamens, stigma, style, carpel, and ovary).
- **5Bs.03** Describe the functions of the parts of a flower (limited to petals, anthers, stigma and ovary).
- **5TWSc.08** Collect and record observations and/or measurements in tables and diagrams appropriate to the type of scientific enquiry.

Background information

Pages 10 and 11 of the *Learner's Book* focus on why plants have flowers and the parts of a flower. The main reason why plants have flowers is for reproduction. Flowers are the reproductive organs of a plant, most are adapted in some way to attract pollinators, some do this by being heavily scented while others use bright colours to attract birds and insects. These adaptations draw pollinators to a particular flower where nectar and pollen is their reward for visiting. Different animals are attracted to different colours; for example, bees are attracted to bright blue and violet while hummingbirds prefer purple, red and pink flowers, butterflies go for red, orange and yellow flowers. Flowers that bloom at night to attract night pollinators do not need brightly-coloured flowers, instead, they use scent to attract animals.

Page 11 focuses on the dissection of a flower to support learners in understanding the formation of a flower and observe and name the different flower parts. Dissection requires learners to apply scientific dispositions such as perseverance and patience as well as close observational skills.

Starter activity suggestions

- Give learners a range of flowers to observe and compare. Ask them which parts they can identify.
- Give learners flowers and an identification book, sheet or key for them to use to identify the name of flowers.
- Take learners outdoors to sketch and/or photograph flowers in the school grounds or maybe a local park. They could use identification keys from the internet or an app to identify and name local flowering plants.
- Tell learners to sort flowers into those with bright colours, scent or both and note which insects or birds are attracted to them.
- Use Unit 1 Slide 5 (boost-learning.com) to revise the of parts of a flower.

Unit 1 Slide 5 answers

Parts of a flowering plant

a

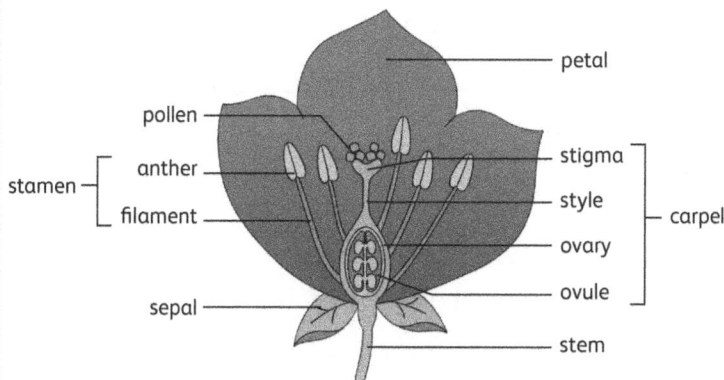

b Learners should note which names they need to research and use books or the internet to find out about each one.

c–d Encourage learners to remember the scientific terms relating to parts of a flower. Give learners time to practise remembering the words and writing them down on a whiteboard. Learners can take turns testing each other.

Activity notes and answers

Page 10 Flowering plants
Activity 1

a Check that learners have compared their flower with the information they have found. Learners should look at features such as colour, shape of petal, and so on.

b Check that learners observe and compare the similarities and differences. Encourage learners to look at the number of petals, scent, what the anthers look like, number of stamens, and so on.

Let's talk

a Example answer: Flowers are brightly coloured to attract insects and birds.

b Example answer: Flowers have a strong scent to attract insects, especially those that are active at night.

Page 11 Parts of a flower

Activity 1

a Check that learners have drawn the different parts of the flower.

b Check that learners have correctly identified the different parts of the flower.

c Listen to discussions and ask learners to share their observations. Encourage learners to take a second and third look at each plant part, each time adding to previous observations so that they become more and more detailed. Offer microscopes or hand lenses to assist learners with looking at the different features. Some learners will find it easier to write the number of each plant part on their page to make pattern-seeking easier. They should see a pattern emerging, for example some parts are double the number of others. This works well if different groups have different flowers so that they can compare the number patterns in parts of each flower. Learners should find a pattern in the number of parts of a flower; usually these are multiples of 2, 3 or 5. Collect the data from learners and display it on the board. Ask learners if the pattern they have found is repeated in different flowers from other groups.

d–e Let learners tape the dissected flowers into their books or onto card. If in books, the flower parts will be pressed and can be used again for revision, such as letting learners compare their flowers.

Activity 2

a This follows on from earlier learning about the flowers that are coloured or scented. The main function of petals is to attract pollinators and to protect the inner parts of the flower.

b Encouraging learners to share what they have found out helps them to articulate learning and to reinforce scientific language and ideas. It also offers access to how well learners understand the functions of parts of a flower.

Further activities

- Invite a florist or a botanist to talk with the class about different flowering plants. They could even work with learners dissecting flowers and teaching them the names and functions of different parts.
- Ask learners to look for other numerical patterns in nature, for example Fibonacci or fractals.
- Challenge learners to find number patterns in flowers in or near their home.
- Use Worksheet 2 (boost-learning.com) to check learners can label the parts of a flower.

ICT links

Learners use the internet to research flower parts and their functions.

Assessment ideas

Engage learners in peer assessing each other on naming different plant parts.

Success criteria

While completing the activities, assess and record learners.

Learning objectives	Success criteria
5Bs.02 Identify the parts of a flower (limited to petals, sepals, anthers, filaments, stamens, stigma, style, carpel, and ovary).	Learners identify parts of the flower they have dissected.
5Bs.03 Describe the functions of the parts of a flower (limited to petals, anthers, stigma and ovary).	Learners can find out the function of a flower's petals.
5TWSc.08 Collect and record observations and/or measurements in tables and diagrams appropriate to the type of scientific enquiry.	Learners can observe the similarities and differences between two plants and record them in a table.

Focus on the male and female parts of a flower

Learner's Book
pages 12–13

Workbook pages 4–5

Visuals 2–3

Learning objectives

- **5Bs.02** Identify the parts of a flower (limited to petals, sepals, anthers, filaments, stamens, stigma, style, carpel, and ovary).
- **5Bs.03** Describe the functions of the parts of a flower (limited to petals, anthers, stigma and ovary).

Background information

The purpose of the activities on pages 12 and 13 of the *Learner's Book* is to develop learners' understanding of the male and female parts of a flower.

Page 12 focuses on the male parts of the flower which includes the stamen. The stamen has two parts: the anther, which makes and stores pollen; and the filament, which is the stalk that holds up the anther.

On page 13 learners learn about the female organ of the flower, the carpel, which has three parts: the stigma, ovary and style. The stigma receives the pollen. The ovary contains ovules, which become seeds after the flower has been fertilised. The style joins the stigma to the ovary.

To get the most out of the activities, make sure learners return to the flower parts that they dissected and use a microscope and/or hand lens to make observations of each part.

Starter activity suggestions

- Revise the names of different parts of a flower using simple games, such as *Put the label on the flower*. Give each group a large flower diagram and labels, when the name of a flower part is called out learners have 10 seconds to decide where it goes on the diagram. Groups get points for correct labelling.
- Give learners jumbled up flower part words and ask them to work as a team to unscramble them.
- Learners write the name of a flower part on their whiteboard; their partner must ask questions to work out which part has been written on their partner's board.

Activity notes and answers

Page 12 The male parts of a flower
Let's talk
Learners should work with a partner to identify the stamen (male part) and the carpel (female part).
Activity 1
a Check that learners have identified the filament and anther correctly.
b Listen to learners' descriptions. For example, a long tube is called a filament and at the end of this is an oval shape with pollen on it, called the anther.
c Check learners' use of the dictionary at the back of the *Learner's Book* to find out what the functions (job) of the anther and the filament are. The anther makes and stores pollen. The filament holds up the anther.
d Check learners' use of the dictionary at the back of the *Learner's Book* to find out what pollen is. Discuss why the pollen is found at the end of the filament.
e This will depend on the types of flowers that the learners have dissected.
Let's talk
a Learners work with their partners to identify the stamens, anthers and filaments (male organs) in each photograph.

b *Similarities*: position (surrounding the carpel), parts (anther and filament).
  Differences: colour, number, shape of anther.
c This could be to attract different pollinators.

Page 13 The female parts of a flower
Activity 1
a Check that learners have identified the carpel correctly and know that it is the female part of the flower.
b Listen to learners' descriptions. For example, the carpel is like a stalk in the centre of the flower. It is, in fact, made up of the stigma, style, ovary and ovules. A carpel is the female part of a flower. Learners might include the ovary at the base with seeds developing inside in some flowers.
c Check learners' use of the dictionary at the back of the *Learner's Book* to find out what the functions (job) of the stigma and the ovary are. The stigma receives the pollen and the ovary becomes the fruit after fertilisation.
d and **e** Listen to learners comparing carpels in different flowers, noting similarities and differences. Their responses will depend on the type of flowers they are observing.

Further activities

Ask learners to complete *Workbook* pages 4 and 5.

Assessment ideas

Use learners' discussions about comparing parts of different flowers as a formative assessment to find out if learners can apply what they know about the male and female parts to different kinds of flowers.

Workbook answers

Page 4 Dissecting a flower
1 Example answers:
  anther – the part of the stamen (male part) that makes (and stores) pollen.
  petal – the parts of the flower that attracts animals such as insects and birds, which can be brightly coloured and scented.
  stigma – part of the carpel where the pollen is received.
  ovary – part of the flower (carpel) where seeds are found.
2 a The pattern is that the sepals and petals are the same number, the stamens are double the number of sepals/petals, and the final number is always 1.
  b Petals: 4, Stamens: 8, Ovary: 1

Page 5 Flower parts
1

Flower part	Information
sepals	the male part of the flower
petals	the female part of the flower
stamen	a powder produced by the male part of the flower
pollen	parts on the outside of the flower
carpel	may be large, brightly coloured, with a pleasant scent (smell)

2 a stamen

b stigma

c protects the flower

3

carpel

pollen

petal

stamen

sepal

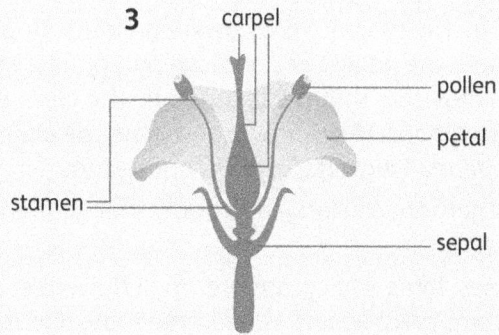

Success criteria

While completing the activities, assess and record learners.

Learning objectives	Success criteria
5Bs.02 Identify the parts of a flower (limited to petals, sepals, anthers, filaments, stamens, stigma, style, carpel, and ovary).	Learners can identify the parts of different flowers: petals, sepals, anthers, filaments, stamens, stigma, style, carpel, and ovary.
5Bs.03 Describe the functions of the parts of a flower (limited to petals, anthers, stigma and ovary).	Learners can recognise and describe the job (function) of the petals, anthers, stigma and ovary of different flowers.

Focus on flowering and non-flowering plants

Learner's Book
pages 14–17

Workbook pages 6–8

Unit 1 Slides 6–8
Unit 1 Flashcards
Visual 4

Unit 1 Audio

Learning objectives

- **5Bs.01** Know that not all plants produce flowers.
- **5Bs.02** Identify the parts of a flower (limited to petals, sepals, anthers, filaments, stamens, stigma, style, carpel, and ovary).
- **5Bs.03** Describe the functions of the parts of a flower (limited to petals, anthers, stigma and ovary).
- **5TWSc.02** Complete a key based on easily observed differences.
- **5TWSm.01** Know that a model presents an object, process or idea in a way that shows some of the important features.
- **5TWSm.02** Use models, including diagrams, to represent and describe scientific phenomena and ideas.

Background information

The purpose of the activities on page 14 of the *Learner's Book* is to apply and consolidate learning about the parts of a flower by challenging learners to create a model flower using recyclable materials. Remind learners that a model is a representation of a real thing and explain that they are making a model flower to help reinforce their learning about the different parts of the flower.

On page 15 learners are introduced to the idea of non-flowering plants. Of the estimated 400 000 species of plants on Earth, the majority are flowering plants. However, there are plants that do not produce flowers to reproduce; these are known as non-flowering plants. These plants grow from spores instead of seeds; spores are very small cells that are released by the plant into the air or water, and when they land in a place with the right conditions, they change and grow to become new plants. Examples of non-flowering plants include mosses, ferns, liverworts, conifers and cycads.

On page 16 learners are challenged to apply their learning in using a key to identify flowering and non-flowering plants.

Liverworts, mosses, ferns and cycads are small flowerless green plants found in moist habitats. Liverworts have leaf-like stems or lobed leaves, lack true roots and reproduce by means of spores released from capsules. Mosses reproduce by means of spores released from stalked capsules.

Ferns have feathery or leafy fronds and reproduce by spores released from the undersides of the fronds. Cycads are palm-like plants that have large male or female cones.

Starter activity suggestions

- Prior to the lesson, ask learners to bring in recyclable materials to use to make their model flowers.
- Discuss the idea of creating a model. Remind learners that it is a replica of the real thing which should look life-like and have as much detail as possible.
- Prior to learners making their model, ensure that they have flowers to observe and compare with what they are making. Give them time to explore the recyclable materials and discuss which items would be suitable for the different parts of the flower.
- Display examples of non-flowering plants such as mosses and ferns. Ferns are particularly useful because the spores can be observed on the underside of the leaves. Provide learners with microscopes and hand lenses to assist with observation.
- Explain how these non-flowering plants differ from flowering plants, and that they do not rely on colourful or scented flowers to attract insects and birds.
- Show learners Slides 6–8 (boost-learning.com) which provide close-up pictures of ferns and mosses. Discuss the differences between non-flowering and flowering plants and explain that when released, the spores will, if conditions are right, grow into new plants.

Activity notes and answers

Page 14 Models and games
Activity 1
As learners make their flower model, visit groups and ask them to explain why they are using specific recyclable items to represent each part. Remind them that the model needs to be accurate and the parts recognisable. Encourage learners to observe the position and shape of each part. Challenge them to pay attention to detail, reminding them that they are working and thinking like scientists and that their model is a copy of a real thing.

Activity 2
The aim of this activity is to help consolidate learning through learners creating a video explaining their model. Challenge learners to use the correct vocabulary and to draft their script before they make their video clip.

Activity 3
This activity provides a cross-curricular link to spelling in the English and ESL curricula. This is another consolidation and application activity. Give learners the opportunity to play their game with another group. A good way for learners to self and peer assess the effectiveness of their game is for another group to play it and then give feedback on how it could help them to learn about parts of a flower. They could also take the game home to play with family members.

Page 15 Do all plants have flowers?
Activity 1
a Use Unit 1 Slides 6–8 (boost-learning.com) to aid discussion. Give learners time to research mosses and ferns and share their findings with other learners.
b Accept appropriate answers that focus on comparing similarities and differences, for example no flowers, spores.
c Example answer: both are green, do not have flowers, have spores.

Activity 2
a stem, leaves, no flowers
b very small and simple
c complex
d fern
e flowers
f ferns

Page 16 Using identification keys for flowering and non-flowering plants
Activity 1
does not look waxy – B Moss
look waxy – C Liverwort
has roots, stems and large leaves – A Ferns
flowering – D Sunflower

Activity 2
a Check learners' identification keys.
b Learners peer assess each other's keys, commenting on whether it works, and if not, they should identify the problem and suggest how to change the key to make it work.

Page 17 What have you learnt about plants?
Activity 1
A anther
B petal
C carpel
D sepal

Activity 2
a Any two: stigma, style, ovary, ovule
b anther, filament

Activity 3
a Petal – The coloured part of a flower that often has a strong scent; attracts insects and birds to pollinate flowers.
b Stigma – The part of the carpel that receives pollen.
c Anther – The part of the stamen that makes and stores pollen.
d Ovary – The part of the carpel that becomes the fruit after fertilisation.

Activity 4
Flowering plants – daisy, dandelion, rose
Non-flowering plants – fern, liverwort, moss

Further activities

- Extend Activities 1 and 3 on page 14 of the *Learner's Book* by asking learners to evaluate the effectiveness of their own model flower and each other's games. They should describe the aspects of the model and games that work well. They then explain what they would do differently next time and why.

- Learners share their information on ferns and mosses with other groups.

- Ask learners to complete *Workbook* pages 6–8.

✏️ **Workbook answers**

Page 6 Working like a botanist

a anther

b ovary

c petals

Page 7 Male and female flower parts

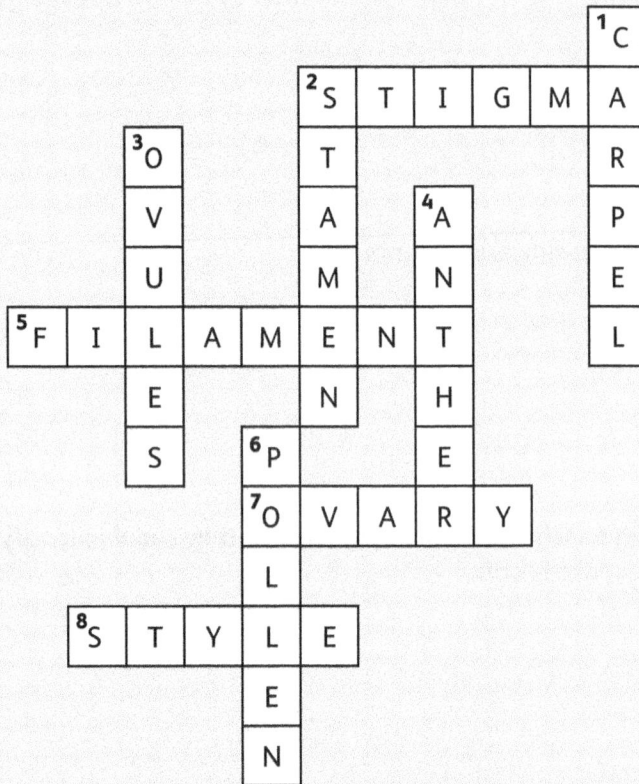

```
                                    ¹C
                    ²S  T  I  G  M  A
          ³O        T                R
           V        A     ⁴A         P
           U        M      N         E
⁵F  I  L  A  M  E  N  T              L
           E        N      H
           S     ⁶P         E
                ⁷O  V  A  R  Y
                 L
⁸S  T  Y  L  E
                 E
                 N
```

Page 8 Flowering and non-flowering plants

1 a Botanists sort plants into two groups: <u>flowering</u> and non-flowering.

   b Some plants, like lilies, have <u>flowers</u> so they are <u>flowering</u> plants.

   c Mosses do not have <u>flowers</u> so they are <u>non-flowering</u> plants.

2 a horsetail

   b fern

   c cycad

3 Give learners the opportunity to share information they have gathered about horsetails and cycads to extend their understanding of these non-flowering plants.

ICT links

Learners can create a video clip about their flower model.

Assessment ideas

- Use the models, games and video clips that learners created as formative assessment evidence of how confident learners are in their knowledge and understanding of parts of flowering plants.
- Use the Flashcards and Audio recordings (boost-learning.com) to assess that learners know and understand the new words and concepts covered in this unit.
- Ask learners to complete the checklist on page 17 of the *Learner's Book*, and the self-check activity on page 9 of the *Workbook*.

Success criteria

While completing the activities, assess and record learners.

Learning objectives	Success criteria
5Bs.01 Know that not all plants produce flowers.	Learners can name non-flowering plants.
5Bs.02 Identify the parts of a flower (limited to petals, sepals, anthers, filaments, stamens, stigma, style, carpel, and ovary).	Learners can identify and name parts of a flower and create a model flower showing the parts.
5Bs.03 Describe the functions of the parts of a flower (limited to petals, anthers, stigma and ovary	Learners can identify and describe the function of the different parts of a flowering plant.
5TWSc.02 Complete a key based on easily observed differences.	Learners can use an identification key to name plants.
5TWSm.01 Know that a model presents an object, process or idea in a way that shows some of the important features.	Learners can use a model of a plant to show the parts of a flower.
5TWSm.02 Use models, including diagrams, to represent and describe scientific phenomena and ideas.	Learners can make a model of a plant to show the parts of a flower.

Unit 2 The life cycle of a flowering plant

Learning objectives overview

Biology	Online resources	LB pages	WB pages	TG pages
Structure and function	Flashcards/Audio			
5Bs.02 Identify the parts of a flower (limited to petals, sepals, anthers, filaments, stamens, stigma, style, carpel, and ovary).	Unit 2 Slide 2	18–19	10–12	33–37
5Bs.03 Describe the functions of the parts of a flower (limited to petals, anthers, stigma and ovary).		18, 22–23		33–37, 37–39
Ecosystems				
5Be.02 Describe how flowering plants are adapted to attract pollinators and promote seed dispersal.		24–26	15–16	39–43
Life processes				
5Bp.02 Know the stages in the life cycle of a flowering plant.	Unit 2 Slides 9–10 Worksheet 4	19–21, 22–23, 24–26, 27–29, 30–31	12–13	33–37, 36–39, 39–43, 43–46, 47–48
5Bp.03 Describe how flowering plants reproduce by pollination, fruit and seed production, and seed dispersal.	Unit 2 Slides 3–6 Unit 2 Video 1	19–21, 22–23, 24–26	12–13, 14, 15–16	33–37, 37–39, 39–43
5Bp.04 Describe seed germination and know that seeds, in general, require water and an appropriate temperature to germinate.	Unit 2 Slide 9 Unit 2 Video 2–3	27–29	17–18	43–46

Thinking and Working Scientifically	LB pages	WB pages	TG pages
Purpose and planning			
5TWSp.02 Know the features of the five main types of scientific enquiry.		13	36–39
5TWSp.03 Make predictions, referring to relevant scientific knowledge and understanding within familiar and unfamiliar contexts.	24, Activity 1 25, Let's talk		39–43
5TWSp.04 Plan fair test investigations, identifying the independent, dependent and control variables.	25, Let's talk 28, Activity 1		39–43, 43–46
Carrying out scientific enquiry			
5TWSc.01 Sort, group and classify objects, materials and living things through testing, observation and using secondary information.	23, Activity 1 25, Activity 1		36–39, 39–42
5TWSc.03 Choose equipment to carry out an investigation and use it appropriately.	25, Let's talk 28, Activity 1		39–43, 43–46
5TWSc.04 Decide when observations and measurements need to be repeated to give more reliable data.	25, Let's talk		39–43
5TWSc.06 Carry out practical work safely.	23, Activity 1	11	36–39
5TWSc.07 Use a range of secondary information sources to research and select relevant evidence to answer questions.	20, Activity 1–2 30, Activity 1		33–37 47–48
5TWSc.08 Collect and record observations and/or measurements in tables and diagrams appropriate to the type of scientific enquiry.	25, Activity 2 28, Activity 1		39–43, 43–46
Analysis, evaluation and conclusions			
5TWSa.01 Describe the accuracy of predictions, based on results.	24, Activity 1 25, Activity 2		39–43
5TWSa.02 Describe patterns in results, including identifying any anomalous results.	28, Activity 2 29, Activity 1		43–46

Analysis, evaluation and conclusions			
5TWSa.03 Make a conclusion from results informed by scientific understanding.	28, Activity 2		43–46
5TWSa.04 Suggest how an investigation could be improved and explain any proposed changes.	28, Activity 2		43–46
5TWSa.05 Present and interpret results using tables, bar charts, dot plots and line graphs.	25, Activity 2 29, Activity 1–2	15	39–43, 43–46

Science in Context	LB pages	WB pages	TG pages
5SIC.03 Use science to support points when discussing issues, situations or actions.	21, Science in context		35
5SIC.05 Discuss how the use of science and technology can have positive and negative environmental effects on their local area.	21, Science in context		35

These learning objectives are reproduced from the Cambridge Primary Science curriculum framework (0097) from 2020. This Cambridge International copyright material is reproduced under licence and remains the intellectual property of Cambridge Assessment International Education.

Cross-curricular links	LB pages	WB pages	TG pages
Mathematics	25, Activity 2 29, Activity 2		41 45
English	20, Activity 1		35
Global Perspectives® Challenge: Will a robot do your job?	21, Activity 1		35

Focus on pollination

Learner's Book
pages 18–21

Workbook pages 10–13

Unit 2 Slides 1–3
Unit 2 Flashcards
Visual 5

Unit 2 Audio

Learning objectives

- **5Bs.02** Identify the parts of a flower (limited to petals, sepals, anthers, filaments, stamens, stigma, style, carpel, and ovary).
- **5Bs.03** Describe the functions of the parts of a flower (limited to petals, anthers, stigma and ovary).
- **5Bp.02** Know the stages in the life cycle of a flowering plant.
- **5Bp.03** Describe how flowering plants reproduce by pollination, fruit and seed production, and seed dispersal.
- **5TWSp.02** Know the features of the five main types of scientific enquiry.
- **5TWSc.07** Use a range of secondary information sources to research and select relevant evidence to answer questions.
- **5SIC.03** Use science to support points when discussing issues, situations or actions.
- **5SIC.05** Discuss how the use of science and technology can have positive and negative environmental effects on their local area.

Background information

The purpose of the activities on page 18 of the *Learner's Book* is to recap learning about the parts of a plant, from Unit 1.

The purpose of the activities on pages 19–21 of the *Learner's Book* is to introduce the process of pollination. The life cycle of a flowering plant is a cyclical (recurring) process, so strictly speaking, there is no beginning.

The *Learner's Book* starts with pollination, which follows on logically from the male and female flower parts in Unit 1.

Pages 19 and 20 focus on pollination explaining how flowers that spread their pollen using pollinators (animals, such as insects, birds and bats) typically have large and/or brightly-coloured petals, and may be scented or produce nectar. Their pollen is spiky, so that it sticks to pollinators. Flowers that use wind to spread their pollen usually have small, dull flowers and no scent. The pollen is small, smooth and light, so the wind can carry it easily.

The *Science in context* activity on page 21 helps learners to explore the global issue relating to the number of insects that are threatened with extinction and the effects. The worst case scenario is that without insects as pollinators life on Earth could disappear, not just plants but also the animals that feed on them. The use of pesticides is a contributing factor to this decline, as is the destruction of habitats. Helping learners to understand the consequences of human action on the natural world is important, as is encouraging them to realise that they can have a positive impact in their own school and home, by for example, growing insect-friendly plants.

Starter activity suggestions

- Display Unit 2 Slide 2 (boost-learning.com). Ask learners to name the numbered plant parts in the diagram.
- Display Unit 2 Slide 3 (boost-learning.com). Discuss the pictures.
- Show learners one or more short video clips of wind carrying pollen. Choose clips that show the plant that is releasing the pollen. Many clips are available online. Ask: *What do you think is happening in the video clips?* Give learners time to discuss their ideas with a partner before taking part in a class discussion.
- If video clips of pollen being carried by the wind are not available, show photographs. If there are any wind-pollinated plants in the school grounds that are at the pollen-producing stage in their life cycle, demonstrate wind pollination directly by tapping the plant lightly to release the pollen.

Unit 2 Slide 2 answers

Parts of a flower

a 1 – stigma 2 – anther 3 – filament 4 – ovary 5 – petal 6 – style

b Give learners a few minutes to check each other's flower part names and spelling.

c It is important that learners know the names of the parts of a plant and can spell them correctly.

Unit 2 Slide 3 answers

Flowers and pollination

a Plants have flowers to attract pollinators so that pollen is transferred from one plant to another (or from one part to another in the same plant).

b 1 – Butterfly is collecting/transferring pollen from another plant. 2 – Hummingbird is collecting/transferring pollen from another plant. 3 – Pollen is being dispersed by wind; the learners should recognise the cloud as being pollen from the plant. 4 – Pollen is being transferred by hand by a human.

c Without pollination fertilisation cannot take place, and plants cannot reproduce (make new plants). This would lead to flowering plants dying out (becoming extinct).

Activity notes and answers

Page 18 Parts of a flower
Activity 1
Check that learners correctly name the parts of their dissected flower. Listen to partners naming parts of the plant. Use this as a formative assessment to check how confident learners are in their knowledge of flower parts.

Activity 2

Learners repeat Activity 1 this time describing the functions of parts of the flower and self/peer assessing what they can remember. Remind learners that if they are unsure, they should find a way to learn and remember the parts and their function.

Page 19 Flower life cycle step 1: pollination
Activity 1

Check that learners have identified the anthers on the flower correctly.

Activity 2

Answers will depend on the kind of flower observed. Check that learners use the magnifying lens correctly to observe the anther and pollen and give appropriate descriptions to their partner.

Page 20 Animals and wind as pollinators
Activity 1

This activity creates cross-curricular links to writing simple sentences in English and ESL.
Example answers:

Bees – Flowers provide bees with nectar and pollen (food). When the bee visits a flower for food, the pollen from the anther sticks to the bee's hairy legs and body and the bee then transfers this to the stigma of another flower.

Hummingbird – As a hummingbird goes from flower to flower feeding on the nectar, the pollen sticks to the hummingbird's beak. When the bird visits a different flower, the pollen is transferred and pollination happens.

Mexican long-tongued bats – They feed on the nectar and pollen of night-blooming flowers; as they go from flower to flower they transfer pollen and pollination happens.

Activity 2

Example answers:

a Insect-pollinated flowers usually have brightly coloured flowers and a strong scent to attract insects with nectar at the base of the flower so that the insect has to brush past the anthers and so will collect pollen.

b Wind-pollinated plants have large anthers that are on the outside. They do not need to be colourful or scented because they do not need to attract insects or birds. The pollen grains are small and light, so that they can be carried easily by the wind. The stigma is often feathery, so it can catch pollen that is carried on the wind.

c They do not have nectar because they are wind-pollinated and do not need to attract insects or birds.

Page 21 Science in context: Why are insect pollinators important?
Activity 1

a Check that learners understand the task and are using their own subject knowledge about pollination as well as research.

b Prior to learners making their video clips, encourage them to storyboard their sequence, writing down their questions and answers. Check that they are factually correct and are using the appropriate scientific language.

c Give learners time to share their video clips with another group. Ask them to give feedback to each other, commenting on the science behind the presentation.

Global Perspectives® Challenge
Will a robot do your job?
Can robots do the job of insect pollinators?

Activity 1 Challenge learners to consider the idea of pollination as a global issue. Ask how scientists could ensure that plants were pollinated. Learners should think about how technology could help, for example, robot insects, drone insects.

Further activities

- At each stage, provide learners with flowers so that they can identify the flower parts and pollen, using a microscope or hand lens to observe.

- Give each pair or group of learners a flower with anthers with pollen. Let them use a cotton bud to role-play an insect visiting their own flower and then transferring pollen from one to the other. This can also represent how humans help the pollination process.

- Start a gardening group, if the school does not already have one, where learners can research and cultivate insect-friendly plants in the school grounds and at home.
- Ask learners to complete *Workbook* pages 10–13.

ICT links

Learners can use the internet to research pollination and different pollinators.

Assessment ideas

- Use the self and peer assessment activities to check learners' prior knowledge of plant parts.
- Use the role play activity to assess if learners understand the process of pollination.

Workbook answers

Page 10 Plant reproduction: flower parts
carpel – the female part of a flower
anther – produces pollen
filament – holds up the anther
style – holds up the stigma and transports the pollen to the ovary
stigma – a female part of the flower that is sticky and collects pollen

Page 11 Sketching parts of a flower
Answers will depend on the flower that learners decide to sketch and research. Check learners' sketches and annotations.

Page 12 Pollination

1 a Pollinated by the wind: wheat, ragweed, saw-tooth oak.
  b Pollinated by animals: orchid, gerbera, jacaranda.

2 Flowers that are pollinated by the wind have small petals. Flowers that are pollinated by animals have large petals.

3 Check learners' drawings and labels.

Page 13 Surveying plants

1 Accept any or all of the following: Observe over time. Pattern seeking. Identify and classify.

2 a Lily
  b Lily because it attracted the most pollinators.
  c Because it was not in flower yet.
  d Accept – It could be because it did not have a scent, only colour in the flowers.

Success criteria

While completing the activities, assess and record learners.

Learning objectives	Success criteria
5Bs.02 Identify the parts of a flower (limited to petals, sepals, anthers, filaments, stamens, stigma, style, carpel, and ovary).	Learners can identify and name each part of the flower.
5Bs.03 Describe the functions of the parts of a flower (limited to petals, anthers, stigma and ovary).	Learners can describe the function (role) of the petal, anthers, stigma and ovary.
5Bp.02 Know the stages in the life cycle of a flowering plant.	Learners can say that pollination is a part of the life cycle of a flowering plant.

Learning objectives	Success criteria
5Bp.03 Describe how flowering plants reproduce by pollination, fruit and seed production, and seed dispersal.	Learners can say that flowers have to be pollinated for reproduction to happen.
5TWSp.02 Know the features of the five main types of scientific enquiry.	Learners can identify the types of scientific enquiry.
5TWSc.07 Use a range of secondary information sources to research and select relevant evidence to answer questions.	Learners research information using the internet.
5SIC.03 Use science to support points when discussing issues, situations or actions.	Learners can use science to discuss why insect pollinators are important.
5SIC.05 Discuss how the use of science and technology can have positive and negative environmental effects on their local area.	Learners can understand the positives and negatives of human action on pollinators.

Focus on plant fertilisation

Learner's Book
pages 22–23

Workbook page 14

Unit 2 Slides 4–5
Visuals 6–7

Learning objectives

- **5Bs.03** Describe the functions of the parts of a flower (limited to petals, anthers, stigma and ovary).
- **5Bp.02** Know the stages in the life cycle of a flowering plant.
- **5Bp.03** Describe how flowering plants reproduce by pollination, fruit and seed production, and seed dispersal.
- **5TWSc.01** Sort, group and classify objects, materials and living things through testing, observation and using secondary information.
- **5TWSc.06** Carry out practical work safely.

Background information

Pages 22 and 23 of the *Learner's Book* focus on developing learners' understanding of the next step in plant reproduction, fertilisation. When a pollen grain is transferred from and lands on the stigma of a flower of the same species, the pollen grain grows a hollow tube (called a pollen tube) down through the centre of the carpel, until it reaches an ovule (egg) inside the ovary.

The nucleus (central part) of the pollen grain then passes along the pollen tube and joins with the nucleus of the ovule. This process is called 'fertilisation'. A fruit only begins to grow after fertilisation has occurred.

Seeds vary widely in size, shape, colour and texture. The world's largest seed belongs to the coco de mer palm. A seed from this plant can reach about 40–50 cm in diameter and can weigh up to 30 kg. Various species of orchids living in tropical rainforests have the world's smallest seeds, with a single seed weighing less than one millionth of a gram.

Starter activity suggestions

- Using real flowers or flowers they have already dissected and stuck into their books, ask learners to locate the ovary. If it is swollen, they could dissect it to see if they can identify seeds.
- Give learners a collection of fruits to dissect and identify. Compare and contrast the different seeds.
- Show learners Unit 2 Slide 4 (boost-learning.com) and discuss how fertilisation takes place.
- Show learners Unit 2 Slide 5 (boost-learning.com) and discuss the questions, reinforcing the difference between a fruit and a seed.

Unit 2 Slide 4 answers

Plant fertilisation

a The pollen grain has come from the anther of another flower (or in some cases the same flower). A bee or other animal (or the wind) transferred the pollen to the stigma.

b The pollen grain produces a pollen tube down to the ovary and finds an ovule (egg) where fertilisation takes place.

c Seed, which if it germinates will grow into a new plant.

Unit 2 Slide 5 answers

Fruits and seeds

a If learners struggle with this question, ask if they have ever seen a fruit with the remains of a flower attached to it, for example a courgette. This may help learners to explain that fruits grow from flowers. Reinforce the difference between a fruit and seed.

b Encourage learners to describe the differences in colour, shape, size, texture and seed placement for each fruit.

c Establish that plants produce seeds in order to reproduce. A new generation of plants grows from the seeds that the parent plant produces.

Activity notes and answers

Page 22 Flower life cycle step 2: fertilisation
Activity 1

Encourage learners to record their observations by taking photographs, sketching or making a video clip. The aim is for them to be able to apply what they have learnt in the classroom in a new context, for example school grounds or local garden. Fruit growth differs from plant to plant, but common changes that occur after fertilisation include swelling of the ovary at the base of the flower and petals dropping.

Work safely ⚠️

Supervise learners' use of a knife. Before learners do this activity, discuss the class rules for using knives safely.

Page 23 Flower life cycle step 3: seed development
Let's talk

The embryo has a food supply to provide food for the roots, shoots and seedling to begin to grow. Once the plant has produced green leaves, it can make its own food.

Activity 1

a–c The responses to this activity will depend on the types of seeds used. Check that learners identify and name the embryo, food supply and seed coat in each seed.

Workbook answers

Page 14 Fertilisation and fruits
The answers will depend on which plants the learners have access to at school or in their own gardens. They should bring their sketches back to class to share. Check that learners have identified the plants, their fruits and how the flower was pollinated. The aim is to begin to draw together the different parts of the life cycle of a plant.

Further activities

- Ask learners to complete *Workbook* page 14.

- Challenge learners to find pictures of the most unusual fruits and seeds produced across the world.

- Give learners fruits to cut in half and ask, for example, *How many different things can you observe? Where are the seeds? What is around the seeds? Why?* Encourage learners to use words such as 'seeds', 'flesh', 'fleshy parts', 'stem' and 'skin' and note similarities or differences in size, colour, texture, fleshy parts, and position of the different parts of the fruits. Learners could record their groupings either by writing a list of the fruits in each group, or by taking photographs of the grouped fruits.

- Ask learners to research plants grown in their own locality or country and find out what the fruits and seeds look like. Remind learners that trees are plants, for example palm tree, dates are the fruits and seeds are inside the date.

- Bring in some unusual fruits that learners might have not tasted and have a tasting session.

- Look at the art of Giuseppe Arcimboldo, an Italian painter, who created portrait heads made from fruits and vegetables. Challenge learners to use images of fruit to create pictures of people or other subjects.

> **Work safely** !
>
> Do not include nuts due to potential food allergies. Check any food allergies or intolerances before any tasting.

Success criteria

While completing the activities, assess and record learners.

Learning objectives	Success criteria
5Bs.03 Describe the functions of the parts of a flower (limited to petals, anthers, stigma and ovary).	Learners can describe the function (role) of the petal, anthers, stigma and ovary.
5Bp.02 Know the stages in the life cycle of a flowering plant.	Learners can say that fertilisation is a part of the life cycle of a flowering plant.
5Bp.03 Describe how flowering plants reproduce by pollination, fruit and seed production, and seed dispersal.	Learners can say that flowers have to be pollinated for fertilisation and seed production to happen.
5TWSc.01 Sort, group and classify objects, materials and living things through testing, observation and using secondary information.	Learners can sort, group and classify seeds.
5TWSc.06 Carry out practical work safely.	Learners know the dangers of using a knife and can use a knife safely.

Focus on seed dispersal

Learner's Book pages 24–26

Workbook pages 15–16

Unit 2 Slide 6
Unit 2 Video 1

> **Learning objectives**
>
> - **5Be.02** Describe how flowering plants are adapted to attract pollinators and promote seed dispersal.
> - **5Bp.02** Know the stages in the life cycle of a flowering plant.
> - **5Bp.03** Describe how flowering plants reproduce by pollination, fruit and seed production, and seed dispersal.
> - **5TWSp.03** Make predictions, referring to relevant scientific knowledge and understanding within familiar and unfamiliar contexts.

- **5TWSp.04** Plan fair test investigations, identifying the independent, dependent and control variables.
- **5TWSc.01** Sort, group and classify objects, materials and living things through testing, observation and using secondary information.
- **5TWSc.03** Choose equipment to carry out an investigation and use it appropriately.
- **5TWSc.04** Decide when observations and measurements need to be repeated to give more reliable data.
- **5TWSa.01** Describe the accuracy of predictions, based on results.

Background information

The purpose of the activities on pages 24–26 of the *Learner's Book* is to introduce and begin to explore the next stage in the life cycle of a flowering plant, seed dispersal. Learners practise making predictions about how a fruit disperses its seeds, based on observations of the physical features of the fruit. Learners have the opportunity to apply a range of scientific enquiry skills through devising and carrying out a fair test to discover which seeds travel furthest in the wind.

Seed dispersal is the next stage in the life cycle of a flowering plant after fertilisation. When plants disperse their seeds, they spread them over a wide area. If all the seeds of a plant fell close to the parent plant, the growing seedlings would have to compete with the parent plant and one another for resources such as water, nutrients, light and space. Very few seedlings would grow to maturity. By spreading their seeds over a wider area, plants increase the chances that each seed will land in a suitable place in which to grow.

One way plants disperse their seeds is by using wind. Page 25 of the *Learner's Book* explores this method. Other methods of seed dispersal are by hooking onto animals' fur; animals eating the seeds (explored on page 26) and passing them in their droppings; exploding; dropping and rolling; being dispersed by water.

Starter activity suggestions

- Play Unit 2 Video 1: Seed dispersal (boost-learning.com). This video shows dandelion seeds being dispersed in the wind.
- Show Unit 2 Slide 6 (boost-learning.com) and discuss the questions about seed dispersal.

Unit 2 Slide 6 answers

Seed dispersal

a To reproduce and produce new plants, to keep the species from becoming extinct.

b Too close to the parent plant and they would compete for space, light, water and nutrients in the soil.

c Explosion – Himalayan balsam. Animals – berries, acorn, burdock. Wind – poppy, dandelion, maple. Water – coconut. (Learners may need more information about how a coconut disperses it's seeds in water. Ask learners to do further research and share their answers in answers in class.)

d No, seeds might not land where there are suitable places to germinate.

e Give learners time to share their research with others in the class.

Activity notes and answers

Page 24 Flower life cycle step 4: seed dispersal
Activity 1

Name of plant	Features of fruit	How the seeds are dispersed
burdock	covered in spikes with hooks on the end	hooks onto animals' fur
grapefruit	large and round	rolls along the ground
water lily	round and flat with holes at the top	carried by water
date	soft and juicy with small seeds	eaten by animals
orchid	splitting open with lots of tiny seeds	carried by the wind
lupin	dry seedpod	explodes
rambutan	covered in spikes/hairs	hooks into animals' fur

Challenge yourself!
Seeds that animals eat are dispersed when the animal passes the seeds in their droppings. By the time the seeds have worked their way through the animal's digestive system, the animal has probably moved a long way from the parent plant.

Page 25 Seed dispersal: wind
Activity 1
Part **a** of this activity would make a good homework activity. Each learner could collect one or two examples of fruits that use wind to disperse their seeds. For part **b**, the class could combine the fruits they collected and work together to sort the fruits into groups.

Let's talk
Using real wind to test their ideas will make it difficult to ensure a fair test as windspeed is unlikely to remain constant. To avoid this, you may want to carry out the investigation indoors using an artificial 'wind' source such as an electric fan. Carrying out repeat readings will ensure a fair test.

Activity 2
This activity creates cross-curricular links to learners' knowledge of interpreting tables and drawing bar charts in Mathematics.

a–c Discuss with learners how best to represent the results shown in the table in a bar chart. You might want to give learners a list of headings you would like them to include in their report. For example, *What we did. How we made sure the test was fair. How we made sure our results are reliable. Results. What the results show.*

d Check that learners can describe how accurate their prediction was, noting that it does not have to be absolutely correct, but how close they think their results are to their prediction.

e Check learners' responses and reasoning.

f The requirement for no more than 100 words is to encourage learners to be concise and precise. Make sure that they describe what they did and explain their results. You might need to remind them of the difference between *describe* and *explain*.

Page 26 More methods of seed dispersal
Activity 1
a–c Answers will depend on which plants learners have chosen. Check learners' description of the method of dispersal and their illustrations of the plant and seed. Give them time to share their fact cards so that their learning about seed dispersal is extended and deepened.

Further activities

- Ask learners to complete *Workbook* pages 15 and 16.

- Learners could collect a range of seeds to bring into school for display. They can sort and identify which plant the seeds belong to, sorting into groups according to methods of dispersal and explore using them to see how they disperse.
- Ask learners to create their own model of a wind-dispersed fruit or seed. Ask them to test their model to find out how far it travels in the wind and compare its performance with the real seeds they have tested.

ICT links

Learners could make a video clip of their seeds dispersing.

Assessment ideas

Learners could sort their collection of seeds in a table to check their understanding of seed dispersal. For example:

Sketch of seed	Name of parent plant	Method of dispersal

Workbook answers

Page 15 Seed dispersal: wind

1 glider – sycamore seeds – stiff wings

parachute – thistle seeds – light fluffy parts

shaker – poppy seeds – openings at the top

2 a A: 273 cm   B: 384 cm   C: 369 cm   D: 291 cm

b B because the average distance travelled was 384 cm, which is further than all of the other seeds.

c Example answers: changed the seed, kept how they measured the same, how they let the seed go the same, repeated readings and calculated averages

Page 16 Methods of seed dispersal

1 Example answers:

Method of seed dispersal	Fruit	What is the evidence?
wind	*dandelion*	*has a parachute*
animals (eaten)	kei apple strawberry	the seeds are in the flesh which animals eat
animals (fur)	cleaver	the seed has hooks to hook onto animal fur
explosion	geranium	it has a spike at the end; when touched, the seed pod explodes
drop and roll	acorns	could drop and roll
water	water lily	the seeds drop into the water

2 They disperse seeds away from the parent plant so that the seed has enough room, light, water and nutrients to grow, so it is not competing with the parent plant or other seedlings.

Success criteria

While completing the activities, assess and record learners.

Learning objectives	Success criteria
5Be.02 Describe how flowering plants are adapted to attract pollinators and promote seed dispersal.	Learners can explain how flowering plants are adapted to promote seed dispersal.
5Bp.02 Know the stages in the life cycle of a flowering plant.	Learners can explain that seed dispersal is part of the life cycle of a flowering plant.
5Bp.03 Describe how flowering plants reproduce by pollination, fruit and seed production, and seed dispersal.	Learners can describe how plants disperse seeds and explain why.
5TWSp.03 Make predictions, referring to relevant scientific knowledge and understanding within familiar and unfamiliar contexts.	Learners can make predictions and suggest how accurate they were.
5TWSp.04 Plan fair test investigations, identifying the independent, dependent and control variables.	Learners can plan and carry out a fair test on seed dispersal.
5TWSc.01 Sort, group and classify objects, materials and living things through testing, observation and using secondary information.	Learners can sort, group and classify seeds according to how they disperse.
5TWSc.03 Choose equipment to carry out an investigation and use it appropriately.	Learners choose their own equipment and use it appropriately when carrying out an activity.
5TWSc.04 Decide when observations and measurements need to be repeated to give more reliable data.	Learners repeat readings and can explain why.
5TWSa.01 Describe the accuracy of predictions, based on results.	Learners can compare their predictions with results and comment on the accuracy.

Focus on germination

Learner's Book
pages 27–29

Workbook pages 17–18

Worksheet 3

Unit 2 Slides 7–8
Unit 2 Video 2–3
Visuals 8–9

Learning objectives

- **5Bp.02** Know the stages in the life cycle of a flowering plant.
- **5Bp.04** Describe seed germination and know that seeds, in general, require water and an appropriate temperature to germinate.
- **5TWSp.04** Plan fair test investigations, identifying the independent, dependent and control variables.
- **5TWSc.03** Choose equipment to carry out an investigation and use it appropriately.
- **5TWSc.08** Collect and record observations and/or measurements in tables and diagrams appropriate to the type of scientific enquiry.
- **5TWSa.02** Describe patterns in results, including identifying any anomalous results.

- **5TWSa.03** Make a conclusion from results informed by scientific understanding.
- **5TWSa.04** Suggest how an investigation could be improved and explain any proposed changes.
- **5TWSa.05** Present and interpret results using tables, bar charts, dot plots and line graphs.

Background information

The purpose of the activity on page 27 of the *Learner's Book* is to introduce the next stage in the life cycle of a flowering plant after seed dispersal – germination. Learners may be familiar with the conditions plants typically need for growth: warmth, water, air, light and a source of nutrients (usually soil). However, learners may not be aware that two of these conditions are not required for seeds to germinate. Seeds do not need soil or light to germinate – only warmth, water and air.

Learners are introduced to the new concepts of germination rates and germination times. Germination rates (the percentage of the total number of seeds planted that germinate) and germination times (the number of days a seed takes to germinate after being planted) depend on the conditions (such as soil temperature and the amount of water). The concept of germination rate creates cross-curricular links to work on percentages in Mathematics.

The investigation on page 28 is to find out the effects of different amounts of water on germination. In order for the investigations to have the desired outcome (to show that seeds can have too much water) you will need to ensure that learners include one group of seeds that are in conditions similar to those that might occur naturally in a flood. (In other words, the soil is completely saturated with standing water on the surface.)

The purpose of the activities on page 29 is to use secondary data as a pattern seeking science enquiry.

Starter activity suggestions

- Watch Unit 2 Video 2: Germination (boost-learning.com). This video shows time-lapse footage of barley grass seeds sprouting. Discuss what learners observe happening.
- Display Unit 2 Slides 7 and 8 (boost-learning.com). Ask learners to discuss the questions on Slide 8 in groups or pairs, and then share their ideas with the rest of the class.
- Give learners Worksheet 3 (boost-learning.com) as a planning framework for their fair test.

Unit 2 Slide 7 answers

Germination

a warmth, air and water
b root
c the embryo
d sunlight (leaves convert sunlight into energy)
e Pictures could show a bean plant with flowers, seed pods, seeds falling out of seed pods.

Unit 2 Slide 8 answers

Different conditions

a Bean in soil in Sun. Soil provides nutrients for the plant and it has Sun (light) for growth/make its own food (photosynthesis).
b Check learners' plans, asking them to share and comment on each other's plans.

Activity notes and answers

Page 27 Flower life cycle step 5: germination
Let's talk

a Listen to learners' responses. Check for understanding and use as a formative assessment, identifying and working with any misconceptions. The correct response is: I think that the roots are the first thing to grow from the seed.

b Learners should be able to suggest a way of testing the idea they have chosen to find out if the idea was correct.

Activity 1

Check learners' plans and their choice of diary. Make sure that they use the correct scientific vocabulary to label their observations. Learners should use their observations to decide which of the ideas was correct and explain why.

Page 28 How water affects germination
Activity 1

a Discuss with learners that they should use more than one set of seeds. Some seeds do not germinate whatever the conditions and this could affect the accuracy of their results.

b Learners should change the volume of water and keep other variables the same, for example type of seed, amount of compost, temperature and light.

c It would be useful to use a range from 0 ml working up in increments of between 10 ml–20 ml so that learners can overwater one set of seeds, to show that a seed can get too much water.

d Refer learners back to the previous activity where they kept a diary of observations and what they are going to record, for example germination time, height of seedlings, colour.

Activity 2

a and b This will depend on the results from each group.

c Accept reasonable answers relating to how each group carried out their investigation. It would be useful to share ideas with the class.

Page 29 How temperature affects germination
Activity 1

a Highest: 20 °C and 25 °C; Lowest: 0 °C and 40 °C

b Shortest: 35 °C; Longest: 15 °C

Activity 2

This activity creates cross-curricular links to interpreting graphs in Mathematics.

a The blue line represents the peas and the orange line represents the melons.

b The blue line (peas) results for 35 °C are anomalous because the pattern of the line was downwards and it suddenly goes up/rises at this point.

Further activities

- Ask learners to complete *Workbook* pages 17 and 18.

- Learners could investigate the germination rate of the same type of seed that is produced by different seed companies to find out which is the best value (do seeds from some companies have a higher germination rate than others?).

- Learners could compare the size of the seeds and the amount of water required to germinate them.

- Watch the Unit 2 Video 3: Daisies growing (boost-learning.com). Discuss what learners observe happening.

Assessment ideas

- Learners could choose to grow flowers or vegetables in a container or plot of ground in the school and create their own seed packet describing how to plant and care for the seeds.

- Learners could write a fiction/non-fiction picture story about seeds germinating for younger learners.

✏️ **Workbook answers**

Page 17 Germination 1

1 Check that learners have labelled the diagram correctly.

2 Seed B because it has water and warmth.

Page 18 Germination 2

1 a Days 12 and 13
  b From day 6 to 16
  c Example: This is a graph to show the number of seeds that germinated over time.

2 a Example answers:
   They changed the amount of light for each set of seeds.
   They kept the type of seed, amount of soil and volume of water the same.
   They measured the number of seeds that germinated.

  b Accept learners' responses. Some might say that they expected seeds to germinate in light, others might say they expected that seeds would germinate in no light.

  c Seeds do not need light to germinate – they need air, warmth and water, so it is not surprising that seeds germinated in the dark.

Success criteria

While completing the activities, assess and record learners.

Learning objectives	Success criteria
5Bp.02 Know the stages in the life cycle of a flowering plant.	Learners can explain that germination is part of the life cycle of a flowering plant.
5Bp.04 Describe seed germination and know that seeds, in general, require water and an appropriate temperature to germinate.	Learners can describe the conditions that a seed needs to germinate such as water, warmth and air.
5TWSp.04 Plan fair test investigations, identifying the independent, dependent and control.	Learners can plan and carry out a fair test investigation involving plants.
5TWSc.03 Choose equipment to carry out an investigation and use it appropriately.	Learners can choose their own equipment and use it appropriately when carrying out an activity.
5TWSc.08 Collect and record observations and/or measurements in tables and diagrams appropriate to the type of scientific enquiry.	Learners can record results from observations using tables.
5TWSa.02 Describe patterns in results, including identifying any anomalous results.	Learners can describe patterns in results and talk about anomalous readings.
5TWSa.03 Make a conclusion from results informed by scientific understanding.	Learners can look at results and make a conclusion.
STWSa.04 Suggest how an investigation could be improved and explain any proposed changes.	Learners can suggest how their investigation can be improved.
5TWSa.05 Present and interpret results using tables, bar charts, dot plots and line graphs.	Learners can interpret and discuss results in graph form.

Focus on life cycle diagrams

Learner's Book
pages 30–31

Workbook page 19

Worksheet 4

Unit 2 Slides 9–10
Unit 2 Flashcards
Visual 10

Unit 2 Audio

Learning objectives

- **5Bp.02** Know the stages in the life cycle of a flowering plant.
- **5TWSc.07** Use a range of secondary information sources to research and select relevant evidence to answer questions.

Background information

Page 30 of the *Learner's Book* focuses on bringing all of the elements in this unit together to develop learners' understanding that the life cycle of a flowering plant can be shown as a diagram from germination to seed production. A life cycle is a cyclical (repeating) process, so life cycle diagrams are usually drawn in the form of a loop. Arrows are used to show how each stage follows on from the next. The stages in the *Learner's Book* diagram are germination, growth, flowering, pollination, fertilisation and seed dispersal.

Starter activity suggestions

Use Unit 2 Slides 9 and 10 (boost-learning.com) to bring together the idea of a life cycle.

Unit 2 Slide 9 answers

The life cycle of a flowering plant

a A plant reproduces, produces seeds, the seeds grow into adult plants, which reproduce, produce seeds, the seeds grow into adult plants and so on – the cycle continues.

b It is called a cycle because it happens over and over.

c Yes, the arrows suggest that the life cycle will happen over and over again.

Unit 2 Slide 10 answers

Growing lettuces

a Give learners time to research hydroponics (a way of growing plants without soil, by using mineral nutrient solutions in water).

b Warmth, water, nutrients, light

c Give learners time to research growing lettuce and to draw the life cycle of a lettuce.

d As a class, plant lettuce seeds to grow through to when they produce seeds. Photograph stages of the life cycle for display.

📄 **Activity notes and answers**

Page 30 Life cycle diagrams
Activity 1
The life cycle diagrams will depend on the flowering plant that learners have chosen to research. Check their diagrams for accuracy and use of correct scientific vocabulary. Learners will need to collect a lot of information about their chosen plant before they draw its life cycle diagram. Learners might collect information through direct observation, talking to adults who know about the plant, looking in books or searching the internet. If learners are not sure which plant to choose, suggest that they choose a plant they like to eat, or a plant growing in the garden at home or at school.

Page 31 What have you learnt about the life cycle of a flowering plant?
Activity 1
a–c Accept reasonable answers.
Activity 2
A fertilisation; B seed dispersal; C seed development; D germination; E pollination
Activity 3
A wind; B drop and roll; C explosion; D water

Further activities

- Groups of learners could create a role play of the life cycle of a flowering plant and perform it for the rest of the class.
- Ask learners to complete Worksheet 4: The life cycle of a dandelion plant (boost-learning.com).

📄 **Worksheet 4 answers**

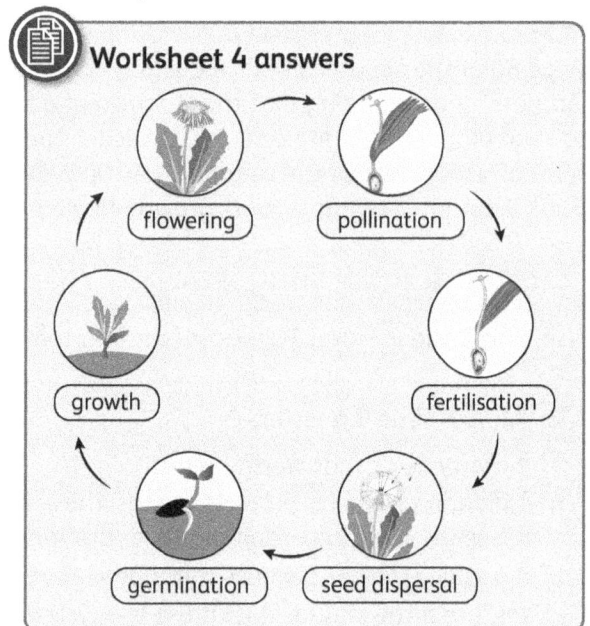

flowering → pollination → fertilisation → seed dispersal → germination → growth → flowering

Assessment ideas

- Use the drawing of life cycle activities to assess understanding of plant life cycles.
- Use the Flashcards and Audio recordings (boost-learning.com) to assess that learners know and understand the new words and concepts covered in this unit.
- Ask learners to complete the checklist on page 31 of the *Learner's Book*, and the self-check activity on page 19 of the *Workbook*.

Success criteria

While completing the activities, assess and record learners.

Learning objectives	Success criteria
5Bp.02 Know the stages in the life cycle of a flowering plant.	Learners can describe the life cycle of a flowering plant.
5TWSc.07 Use a range of secondary information sources to research and select relevant evidence to answer questions.	Learners carry out research using the internet on the life cycle of a flowering plant.

Unit 3 Adaptation

Review of prior learning

Learning objectives from Stages 1–4	LB pages	WB pages	TG pages
4Be.01 Know that different animals are found in, and suited to, different habitats.	32		50–52
4Be.03 Describe food chains as being made of producers and consumers, and classify consumers as herbivores, omnivores, carnivores, predators and/or prey.	32		50–52

Learning objectives overview

Biology	Online resources	LB pages	WB pages	TG pages
Ecosystems	Flashcards/Audio			
5Be.01 Describe how plants and animals are adapted to environments that are hot, cold, wet and/or dry.	Unit 3 Slides 1–4 Worksheets 5–6	33, 34–35, 42–43	21–22	50–52, 53–55, 63–64
5Be.03 Describe the common adaptations of predator and prey animals.	Unit 3 Slides 5–7	36–37, 38–39, 40–41, 42–43	24, 25, 26	55–57, 58–60, 60–62, 63–64

Thinking and Working Scientifically	LB pages	WB pages	TG pages
Models and representations			
5TWSm.01 Know that a model presents an object, process or idea in a way that shows some of the important features.	41, Activity 1 and 3 42, Activity 2		60–62, 63–64
5TWSm.02 Use models, including diagrams, to represent and describe scientific phenomena and ideas.	41, Activity 1 and 3 42, Activity 2	27	60–62, 63–64
Purpose and planning			
5TWSp.01 Ask scientific questions and select appropriate scientific enquiries to use.	35, Activity 1		53–55
Carrying out scientific enquiry			
5TWSc.07 Use a range of secondary information sources to research and select relevant evidence to answer questions.	34, Activity 2 35, Activity 1 36, Activity 1 37, Activity 1 38, Activity 1		53–54, 55–57, 58–60

Science in Context	LB pages	WB pages	TG pages
5SIC.03 Use science to support points when discussing issues, situations or actions.	40		61

These learning objectives are reproduced from the Cambridge Primary Science curriculum framework (0097) from 2020. This Cambridge International copyright material is reproduced under licence and remains the intellectual property of Cambridge Assessment International Education.

Cross-curricular links	LB pages	WB pages	TG pages
English	35, Activity 1 37, Activity 1	21	54 56

Focus on adaptation

Learner's Book
pages 32–33

Workbook page 20

Worksheet 5

Unit 3 Slides 1–3
Unit 3 Flashcards

Unit 3 Audio

Learning objectives

Revision of:

- **4Be.01** *Know that different animals are found in, and suited to, different habitats.*
- **4Be.03** *Describe food chains as being made of producers and consumers, and classify consumers as herbivores, omnivores, carnivores, predators and/or prey.*
- **5Be.01** Describe how plants and animals are adapted to environments that are hot, cold, wet and/or dry.

Background information

The activity on page 32 of the *Learner's Book* aims to elicit learning about plants, animals and their habitats from Stage 4. Learners use a grid and answer questions which are set to prompt learners' memory relating to prior learning. Encourage learners to share ideas and discuss what they know, and to change their ideas as they begin to make sense of past learning.

Page 33 introduces the concept of adaptation (that plants and animals have special features or ways of behaving that help them to survive by adjusting to new environments or changes in their current environment). The most useful adaptations are passed on to the next generation; plants and animals that are unable to adapt may become extinct.

Starter activity suggestions

- Ask the class if they already know anything about the words 'adapt' and 'adaptation'. Scribe their ideas and display them on, for example, a working wall. Return to these at the end of this unit and ask learners to reconsider their definitions and possibly write new ones.
- Ask learners to share what they know about animals and plants that have adapted to their environment.
- Use the photographs on the introductory Unit 3 Slide 1 (boost-learning.com) to prompt discussion and elicit what learners know about adaptation.
- Use Unit 3 Slide 2 (boost-learning.com) for reflection on science learning.

Unit 3 Slide 1 answers

The Venus Fly Trap plant has adapted to get nutrients from insects; it has sensitive hairs on leaves which when triggered result in the leaves shutting and trapping the insect which it then digests.

The lion is camouflaged in the grass so that its prey cannot see it.

Wolves work as a group in a pack to hunt, so that they can be more successful in finding food.

Seahorses have adapted so that they use camouflage by changing colour to match their habitat.

Unit 3 Slide 2 answers

Sharing what you know about living things

a Encourage learners to reflect on how they learn in science, so that they recognise that sharing ideas is positive and helps them to remember or change some of their thinking.
b Listen to learners, using this as formative assessment to identify misconceptions.
c This is a fun starter activity. Usually the phrase or sentence whispered is not the same by the time it has travelled round the class. Make sure that the first statement is one about living things. At the end, the last person says what they heard out loud and learners have to work out what the original statement was.

📄 Activity notes and answers

Page 32 Sharing what you know
Activity 1

a and **b** Give learners the time to research answers using the internet and to use the dictionary at the back of the *Learner's Book*.

Example answers:

A habitat is where a plant or animal lives, the environment is the wider area and includes everything including the weather.

A carnivore is an animal that eats other animals.

Herbivores, for example cows, elephant, zebra, tortoises, caterpillars, finches.

Omnivores are animals that eat other animals and plants.

Check that learners' food chains begin with producer (plant), prey and predator.

Sea – whale, octopus, turtle, sea slug, dolphins, krill, cuttlefish.

Rainforest – macaw, mountain gorilla, boa constrictor, sloth, poison dart frog, jaguar.

Desert – cacti, date palm, thyme, wild desert gourd, scorpion, kangaroo rat, oryx, sand fox, secretary birds, chameleons, skunks.

c–e To help develop reflective learners, give them time to share with other groups, act upon comments to improve their answers, and think about what they already know and what they found difficult and why.

Page 33 What is adaptation?
Activity 1

A small seeds – **3** are easily dispersed by the wind

B thin leaves – **1** reduce water loss from the plant

C not very tall – **2** protect from strong cold winds

D fluffy white tufts – **5** traps solar heat to keep the plant warm when the climate is cold

E produces seeds quickly – **4** makes the most of the short, warm summer growing season

Further activities

- Create a working wall onto which learners place fascinating facts about plants and animals and their adaptations.

- Put learners into groups where they are a specialist animal, for example tree-living, underground expert, adapted for flying, pack hunters, swimmers. Each group should research their specialist animals and over the course of the unit collect information to communicate to the rest of the class as a PowerPoint, poster, role play or display.

- Show learners Unit 3 Slide 3 (boost-learning.com) and discuss their ideas, then ask them to complete Worksheet 5 (boost-learning.com) either in class or as a research project at home.

- Ask learners to complete *Workbook* page 20.

📄 Worksheet 5 answers

Horns – used for fighting with other giraffes and against predators
Long tongue – helps rip leaves off trees
Tough lips – used to protect lips from thorns of trees
Long neck – used to reach leaves on taller trees
Long legs – helps reach leaves for food and protect against predators
Hooves – tough to protect feet and against predators
Fringed tail – swats insects and flies away
Camouflaged coat – colours and pattern helps to camouflage so it is harder to see by predators

✐ Workbook answers

Page 20 Adaptations

1 a An adaptation is a special feature or way of behaving that help plants and animals to survive by adjusting to new environments or changes in their current environment. For example: camouflage and pack hunting.

   b Physical adaptations is an adaptation made to the body of an animal to ensure its survival. For example, a polar bear's thick layer of fat and a lion's retractable claws.

   c Behaviour adaptations is an adaptation to the way an animal behaves. For example, pack hunting and ambush.

2 a Red caterpillars because they are not well camouflaged and the colour sticks out.

   b Green caterpillars because they are well camouflaged.

   c Because the colour red is easily seen so most of these caterpillars would have been found quickly.

   d Gradually the eyes would accustom to looking for the different colours and the green would begin to be seen.

   e The best camouflaged was the green and the worst camouflaged was the red. The least amount of green was found and the most amount of red was found.

   f Because the caterpillar uses the colour to warn predators that they are unpleasant/dangerous/poisonous to eat.

ICT links

Learners use the internet at home to research more information on adaptation and how different animals and plants have adapted to suit their environment.

Assessment ideas

- Use the activities on page 32 of the *Learner's Book* to assess prior understanding from Stage 4, checking that learners are confident in key ideas.
- Use a working wall to collect learners' ideas and work and use it to track progress through this unit.

Success criteria

While completing the activities, assess and record learners.

Learning objectives	Success criteria
4Be.01 *Know that different animals are found in, and suited to, different habitats.*	Learners can say which animals live in different habitats and how they are suited to live there.
4Be.03 *Describe food chains as being made of producers and consumers, and classify consumers as herbivores, omnivores, carnivores, predators and/or prey.*	Learners can create different food chains and say which are consumers, producers, predators, prey, herbivores, omnivores and carnivores.
5Be.01 Describe how plants and animals are adapted to environments that are hot, cold, wet and/or dry.	Learners can describe how a plant is adapted to a cold environment.

Focus on adaptations in cold and hot environments

Learner's Book
pages 34–35

Workbook pages 21–23

Visuals 11–13
Unit 3 Slide 4

Learning objectives

- **5Be.01** Describe how plants and animals are adapted to environments that are hot, cold, wet and/or dry.
- **5TWSp.01** Ask scientific questions and select appropriate scientific enquiries to use.
- **5TWSc.07** Use a range of secondary information sources to research and select relevant evidence to answer questions.

Background information

The aim of pages 34 and 35 of the *Learner's Book* is to introduce learners to adaptations relating to environments that are cold and hot. Animals living in, for example, polar regions have developed a range of adaptations, such as white fur as camouflage against the snow and ice. Thick fur or two layers of fur and layers of fat (blubber) help to insulate against the cold, while small ears ensure that large areas of skin are not exposed to low temperatures. Some animals have large feet (polar bears) or wide hooves (musk oxen) that act like snowshoes enabling them to walk across snow without sinking in.

Plants in these regions are not tall, but low growing to avoid strong, icy winds. Some are hairy to trap the heat, such as Arctic poppies. The flower of this plant can track the Sun so the plant can make the most of the short periods of light to photosynthesise.

In very hot environments such as deserts, adaptations relate to keeping cool and preventing water loss. Animals do this by burrowing under the ground, where is it cooler and damper. They stay there during the day, coming out to feed at night when temperatures are cooler. Water is scarce in these regions, so most animals get their water from animals and plants that they eat. Animals such as spiders and scorpions have a thick outer covering, which helps to reduce the water lost from the body. Plants have also adapted to these environments. Their roots are often just under the soil and spread out a long way. When it rains, they can take up as much water as possible, while leaves have a waxy coat to stop water from being lost. They store water in their roots or the leaves and stems.

Starter activity suggestions

- Show learners photographs of different plants and animals that live in both desert and polar regions. Ask them to look for similarities and differences between them and suggest reasons.
- Get learners to imagine that they are scientists going to live in the desert or polar regions. Are human bodies able to adapt to those environments? What adaptations would they give humans?

Activity notes and answers

Page 34 Adaptations to different habitats
Activity 1
b white fur – camouflage against the ice and snow
  large, rough, sandpaper-like paws – gripping ice and to prevent sinking into the ice
  big claws – gripping on ice and to catch prey
  thick layer of fat under the skin – insulation to keep warm
  small ears – to reduce heat loss
  small tail – to reduce heat loss
  good sense of smell – so that they can smell prey many miles away and under ice (they can smell a seal nearly 30 kilometres away)

Activity 2

a Refer learners back to to the photograph on page 33 to compare to the rainforest habitat. For example: A rainforest is hot and wet with many large plants.

b Rainforest plants have:

Drip tips – plants have leaves with pointy tips so water can run off the plant.

Tall tree trunks to reach the light where there is a lot of competition because there are so many trees, they are all trying to get to the light.

Trees have smooth bark so that the water runs down easily to the roots.

Big buttress roots that help to support the tall trees, stopping them from falling over.

Some plants are vines so that they can climb up trees to the light.

Page 35 Animals and plants adapted to live in hot environments

Activity 1

The use of question stems creates cross-curricular links to English and ESL.

a–d Support learners by modelling how questions stems are used. Ensure that learners ask a range of question types, for example: *How are cacti adapted to survive without water? When do they flower?*

This activity provides an excellent opportunity for learners to use ICT skills to represent information, for example a leaflet, poster, PowerPoint slide, newspaper article, podcast or video clip.

Further activities

- Give learners the opportunity to display or share their work with other groups or the rest of the class.
- Create a collage of one or more of the habitats, for example rainforest and a desert, comparing and contrasting adaptations. Learners could create camouflaged animals, vine plants that reach the canopy and place animals where they live, for example the forest floor or the top of the canopy.
- Show learners Unit 3 Slide 4 (boost-learning.com) about a water lily and discuss the questions.
- Ask learners to complete *Workbook* pages 21–23.

Unit 3 Slide 4 answers

Plant adaptations in water

a–c Learners' own ideas about water lily adaptations, and so on.

d Learners do research to check their answers and how good their scientific thinking was. Ask learners to present their findings to the class.

Workbook answers

Page 21 Plant adaptations

1 a Example: The giant water lily has a flat shape so it floats on the surface of the water and it is big so it gets lots of light.

b Example: The giant water lily has spines on the bottom of the leaves to protect itself from fish and other predators that might want to eat it.

2 a

Habitat	Plant	Adaptation
Desert	2	A
Arctic	3	B
Savannah	1	C

Page 22 Fish adaptations

1 Example: To make it harder for predators to eat the fish.

2 Example: So that they can move through water more quickly to catch prey, or to avoid predators.

3 Example: To scare away and confuse predators.

4 Check learners' answers.

Page 23 Work out why

1 Everyone in the mob participates in gathering food, keeping a look out for predators and taking care of the babies, so they all benefit.

2 So that they can survive low temperatures.

3 They do not drink water because they have adapted to be able to survive in deserts where there is little or no water for long periods of time.

4 So that the mother can call her calf without other animals hearing it and alerting them to the baby okapi which would put it in danger of being found by a predator.

Assessment ideas

Learners could engage in a 'hot seat' session where the rest of the class ask questions about the animal they have researched and the person in the seat answers them. This provide a good opportunity to listen to learners and carry out a formative assessment on how well their understanding of adaptation is developing.

Success criteria

While completing the activities, assess and record learners.

Learning objectives	Success criteria
5Be.01 Describe how plants and animals are adapted to environments that are hot, cold, wet and/or dry.	Learners can describe how plants and animals are adapted to different environments.
5TWSp.01 Ask scientific questions and select appropriate scientific enquiries to use.	Learners can ask questions about adaptation.
5TWSc.07 Use a range of secondary information sources to research and select relevant evidence to answer questions.	Learners can research information about adaptation and use it to answer questions.

Focus on predator adaptations

Learner's Book
pages 36–37

Workbook page 24

Worksheet 6

Unit 3 Slide 5
Visual 14

Learning objectives

- **5Be.03** Describe the common adaptations of predator and prey animals.
- **5TWSc.07** Use a range of secondary information sources to research and select relevant evidence to answer questions.

Background information

Page 36 of the *Learner's Book* aims to introduce learners to the idea that predators are adapted to hunt, kill and eat prey for food. These adaptations can be physical as well as in the way the animals behave.

A common set of predator adaptations are strong teeth, claws and jaws, for example in wolves, tigers and lions; however, the household cat has these as well. Other animals have different adaptations for hunting; for example, eagles have large talons for catching and holding food and sharp hooked beaks for tearing. On page 37 the aim is to illustrate how some animals have adapted their behaviour to catch food, for example, wolves hunt in packs, they do this because it allows them to work together to bring down larger prey such as a moose or bison.

The activities focus on learners researching information using books, the internet or video clips to develop their understanding and represent what they find out in different ways. Discuss with learners what makes a good information search, for example focusing on key words, such as 'adaptation', 'predator', 'prey'. They should be selective and take notes on key points, rather than copying everything they read. When they are presenting their research, encourage learners to think about their audience; for example, what are the important points they should know, and what might be interesting to them.

Starter activity suggestions

- Show Unit 3 Slide 5 (boost-learning.com) and discuss how the peregrine falcon is adapted to hunt for prey. Remind learners that animals need to feed to survive, so adapting to become more successful at hunting is important.

- Discuss with learners how to be more effective when researching information. Collect their suggestions and display them on a working wall or the interactive whiteboard.

- Discuss with learners how to be an effective communicator, so that others will find their work interesting and learn from it. Ask them to think about when they have learnt something new. How was it presented, did it catch their eye, how was it explained so that they understood and remembered the information?

Unit 3 Slide 5 answers

Predator adaptations – peregrine falcon

Photograph 1 – Peregrine falcons can pull their claws in as they fly and have excellent vision to see prey from high up.

Photograph 2 – Peregrine falcons can bring their wings back to create a streamlined shape that allows them to move through the air at great speed.

Photograph 3 – Peregrine falcons have large sharp talons for catching and gripping prey.

Photograph 4 – Peregrine falcons have sharp talons and a hooked beak for tearing meat off the carcass.

Activity notes and answers

Page 36 Predator adaptations
Activity 1

a–d Use the *Starter activity suggestions* to support learners in research and presenting information. Give learners time to draft and redraft their poster to make information accessible and interesting for others to read. Once the posters are complete, display them so that learners can visit each one to extend their learning about predator adaptations. Give each learner a 'sticky note' so that they can leave constructive comments, such as what they found interesting or like about the poster and a suggestion for what could be improved.

Page 37 Adapting behaviour
Activity 1

This activity creates cross-curricular links to writing in English and ESL.

- Common name: Orca whales are also known as killer whales.
- Latin name: *Orcinus orca*
- Habitat: Orcas can be found in each of the world's oceans.
- Prey: They eat fish, squid, seals, penguins and other whales.

- Behavioural adaptations to improve hunting: Orcas will work together in groups called pods to hunt prey. They herd fish and stun them with their tails. They can also work together to make waves that throw prey off floating ice.
- Physical adaptations for hunting: Orcas are black and white to camouflage them in the water, they have blubber to keep them warm in polar seas, their shape means they can glide through water and they have sharp teeth to rip and chew prey.
- Fascinating fact: Orcas are not really whales; they are dolphins.

Further activities

- Ask learners to complete *Workbook* page 24.
- Create an amazing fact book about orcas or predator adaptations for learners to add to. They should add facts they have found out about at school or at home.
- Give learners Worksheet 6 (boost-learning.com) to create fact files about animal adaptations.

Home/school activity

Learners could start making their own 'Fact or Top Trumps' cards using Worksheet 6 (boost-learning.com) at home, choosing their own animals and plants to research and sharing or swapping them with others in the class.

ICT links

Support learners in using the internet to research how other animals have adapted to be successful predators. Provide a list of useful websites including video clips.

Assessment ideas

Use these activities as opportunities to assess learners' ability to research scientific information and ideas using secondary information sources as well as their ability to apply literacy skills in science.

Workbook answers

Page 24 Predator adaptations

1 Example answer: To be successful hunters and ensure they have food to eat.
2 a Stalking: polar bears, lions, great white sharks, Komodo dragons
  b Hunting in a pack (group): wolves, lions, dolphins, spotted hyenas
  c Teeth and claws: hawks, eagles, cats
3 Cats have retractable claws to use when hunting. They use them to grip the ground, climb trees and catch prey. Then they retract the claws to protect them against wear and tear, and to keep them sharp.

Success criteria

While completing the activities, assess and record learners.

Learning objectives	Success criteria
5Be.03 Describe the common adaptations of predator and prey animals.	Learners can describe different predator adaptations.
5TWSc.07 Use a range of secondary information sources to research and select relevant evidence to answer questions.	Learners use a range of secondary sources to research information on predator adaptations.

Focus on prey adaptations

Learner's Book
pages 38–39

Workbook page 25

Worksheet 7

Unit 3 Slide 6

Learning objectives

- **5Be.03** Describe the common adaptations of predator and prey animals.
- **5TWSc.07** Use a range of secondary information sources to research and select relevant evidence to answer questions.

Background information

Adaptations help animals to survive; prey adaptations help animals avoid being eaten by predators. Animals have adapted in different ways, some use camouflage to help them blend in with their surroundings, such as the walking leaf insect and some caterpillars. Others have a highly developed sense of smell or sight, for example, the African bush elephant can smell food that is several miles away as well as potential predators such as lions.

The activities on pages 38 and 39 of the *Learner's Book* focus on prey adaptations, illustrating the range of ways in which animals have adapted to avoid being caught and eaten. Learners also continue to develop their research skills, a feature of this unit, along with their skills of communicating information.

Starter activity suggestions

- Show learners Unit 3 Slide 6 (boost-learning.com) and ask them to work with their partner to answer the questions. Encourage learners to think through answers logically, using what they know about predators and the information given on the slide.
- Ask learners to think of animals that they know about and how they avoid being eaten by a predator. Share ideas around the class.

Unit 3 Slide 6 answers

Jerboa adaptations

a To avoid predators and because it is cooler underground.

b It gets water from the plants and insects it eats.

c Stops sand from being breathed in.

d To stop sand getting into its ears and damaging its hearing which they use to listen for predators.

e To enable it to escape predators by running or jumping.

f To prevent heat getting in.

g For feeling around in the dark at night and in burrows.

h To confuse predators so that they will not know in which direction the jerboa is moving.

Activity notes and answers

Page 38 Prey adaptations
Activity 1
a–c The answers will depend on learners' research. Examples have been provided in the table on the next page. Give learners time to plan out their poster, discuss what makes a good poster.

Prey adaptation	Animal name	Habitat	What the adaptation is like	Name of some of the animal's predators
camouflage	*grasshopper*	*grassland*	*The grasshopper is a green colour, the same colour as the grass so that it is harder for its prey to see it.*	birds and snakes
burrowing	rabbit	grassland	The rabbit is a similar colour to the grass, burrow provides escape from predators.	foxes and owls
spikes	porcupines echidnas sea urchins	deserts grasslands and forests sea	All expose the spikes to predators.	lizards, foxes eagles, owls sea otters, lobsters, birds
hearing	elephants antelopes	grassland grassland and forests	Elephants have a hearing range of over 3 km. They can hear predators during the day and after dark.	lions, hyenas and humans lions and cheetahs
alarm calls/ warning signals	meerkats	deserts and grasslands	Sentries send out high pitched warning squeals.	eagles, hawks and jackals
feeding at night	small rodents such as mice aye aye	grass and woodlands rainforests of Madagascar	Feed at night to avoid being easily seen. To avoid predators.	birds of prey, snakes fossa (cat-like mammal), birds of prey
speed	Thomson's gazelle		Reaches speeds of up to 80 km/h to avoid prey.	lions, hyenas, wild dogs and jackals

d Discuss the points and ask learners to think about other ways that they could make their poster eye-catching and interesting.

Page 39 More prey adaptations
Activity 1
a Their bright colours warn other animals that they are poisonous.
b So that it can warn animals to stay away.
c The fire-bellied snake has developed resistance to the poison.

Activity 2
a They have stinging tentacles and their transparent bodies help them hide.
b Tuna fish, sharks, sea turtles and penguins eat jellyfish.

Activity 3
a It uses its horns to attack lions.
b A pride of lions will attack from different sides of the buffalo, which means at least one of them can badly injure it and the others help to bring it down.

Activity 4
a It has a thick strong shell into which it withdraws its head and limbs when threatened. It also blends into its surroundings; its colour camouflages it. Tortoises also have strong claws and burrow into the ground to avoid predators.
b Ravens and Gila monsters (venomous lizards), foxes.
c Bite through their shells, pull off legs, eat their eggs and young.

Further activities

- Ask learners to complete *Workbook* page 25.
- Learners could go back and use Worksheet 7 (boost-learning.com) to create new fact files on animals that they have been researching. These could form part of a home/school activity.
- Give learners the opportunity to pair up and share information on the same or different animals, to broaden their knowledge of adaptations.

ICT links

Learners could create a 'tweet' of 140 characters about adaptation, or a specific animal.

Assessment ideas

- Ask learners to write down the three most interesting things that they learnt from the activities.
- Challenge groups to write a quiz about adaptation for another group, which they have to mark and explain the correct answer where a group has made a mistake.

Workbook answers

Page 25 Prey adaptations

1 Rattlesnake – D   2 Whitetailed deer – C
3 Skunk – A   4 Praying mantis – H
5 Beaver – B   6 Porcupine – E
7 Pronghorn – F   8 Japanese tit – G

Success criteria

While completing the activities, assess and record learners.

Learning objectives	Success criteria
5Be.03 Describe the common adaptations of predator and prey animals.	Learners can describe different prey adaptations.
5TWSc.07 Use a range of secondary information sources to research and select relevant evidence to answer questions.	Learners use a range of secondary sources to research information on prey adaptations.

Focus on Darwin's finches

Learner's Book
pages 40–41

Workbook page 26

Unit 3 Slide 7
Visual 15

Learning objectives

- **5Be.03** Describe the common adaptations of predator and prey animals.
- **5TWSm.01** Know that a model presents an object, process or idea in a way that shows some of the important features.
- **5TWSm.02** Use models, including diagrams, to represent and describe scientific phenomena and ideas.
- **5TWSp.04** Plan fair test investigations, identifying the independent, dependent and control variables.
- **5SIC.03** Use science to support points when discussing issues, situations or actions.

Background information

Page 40 of the *Learner's Book* is a *Science in context* activity that focuses on the work of the scientist Charles Darwin who, when he visited the Galapagos Islands observed that there were different kinds of finches on each island. He noticed that the beaks were adapted to eat the different foods that were available, such as seeds, nectar and insects.

Darwin called his idea *Natural Selection*, the concept that animals needed to adapt to changes in their habitats. If they failed to do so, they would die out, becoming extinct.

The aim of the activities on page 41 is for learners to model different beaks and which food they are adapted to eat, modelling Darwin's idea of Natural Selection. Some learners will find that their 'beak' is not adapted to feed on certain kinds of food. Discuss with learners that the activity models Darwin's idea so that they are able to understand it.

Starter activity suggestions

- Before the lesson set a home/school activity where learners research Charles Darwin and bring five key facts about him to the lesson. Give learners time to share what they have found out. Display common facts on the whiteboard or working wall.
- Use Unit 3 Slide 7 (boost-learning.com) and discuss the questions. Develop the idea that the birds are all finches but have different beaks, then link it to the idea that they eat different kinds of food.

Unit 3 Slide 7 answers

Darwin's finches

a The birds look the same but have different shaped beaks.

b The beaks are different shapes and sizes. They are adapted to eat different food.

c No, because their beaks are different.

d Beak 1 is a thick big beak the bird might eat big seeds and nuts, because the beak can crack it. Beak 2 is not as big and so the bird might eat smaller seeds and berries. Beak 3 is very small so the food will have to be smaller, such as small seeds. Beak 4 is pointed so the bird might eat insects, as it might spear them.

Activity notes and answers

Page 40 Science in context: Darwin's finches
Let's talk
Parrot – *nutcracker* for cracking nuts and seeds
Peregrine falcon – *hook* for tearing flesh
Woodpecker – *chisel* to find insects that are hidden
Stork – *spear* for catching fish in streams

Page 41 Role-playing bird beak adaptations
Activity 1
Learners carry out the instructions, collect data and should conclude that one type of beak that they are modelling is less effective for eating food than the other.
Activity 2
The answers will depend on their results, but the idea is that learners use the model to decide which beak is best adapted to which food. Discuss with the class their results, and how modelling different beaks helps them to understand that if they did not have a beak that would pick up one of the foods, they could 'die' of starvation.

Activity 3

Modelling using a different beak each to eat the macaroni should show that one type of beak is less effective than the other. Ask learners to think about what Darwin would have concluded from this activity and if it supported his theory about Darwin's finches and natural selection.

Further activities

- Challenge learners to identify four birds in their locality and sketch the head of the bird showing the beak. Ask them to predict what kind of food it eats from the shape of its beak. They then research what each bird eats to find out if they were correct.
- Ask learners to complete *Workbook* page 26.

ICT links

Learners could use a bird identification app to identify each bird.

Assessment ideas

Ask learners to write down 3 things that they have learnt from the activities about Darwin's finches, 2 words and 1 idea that they think is the most important to learn.

Workbook answers

Page 26 Beaky Island bird adaptations

1 a The chopstick beak because it ate the most amount of spiders.
 b Clothespin because it ate the least amount of insects.
 c worms: tweezers; greenfly: spoon
 d The spoon beak bird might become extinct because it was not able to pick up many worms (less than 5), but the tweezer beak bird would be very successful as its numbers were the highest for worms (over 25).
 e Scissors and tweezers because their beaks caught the least spiders.
 f The tweezer because worms are a similar shape to caterpillars.
 g Accept reasonable answers. Example: *Tweezer because it was able to catch some of each insect.* Some learners might say that the chopstick might not survive because it could only catch mainly spiders.

Success criteria

While completing the activities, assess and record learners.

Learning objectives	Success criteria
5Be.03 Describe the common adaptations of predator and prey animals.	Learners can talk about how bird beaks are adapted to suit the food available.
5TWSm.01 Know that a model presents an object, process or idea in a way that shows some of the important features.	Learners can describe how using chopsticks, and so on, models Darwin's ideas about beaks and natural selection.
5TWSm.02 Use models, including diagrams, to represent and describe scientific phenomena and ideas.	Learners can describe how using chopsticks, and so on, models Darwin's ideas about beaks and natural selection.
5SIC.03 Use science to support points when discussing issues, situations or actions.	Learners can explain Darwin's theory of natural selection.

Focus on discovering a new animal

Learner's Book
pages 42–43

Workbook pages 27–28

Unit 3 Flashcards

Unit 3 Audio

Learning objectives

- **5Be.01** Describe how plants and animals are adapted to environments that are hot, cold, wet and/or dry.
- **5Be.03** Describe the common adaptations of predator and prey animals.
- **5TWSm.01** Know that a model presents an object, process or idea in a way that shows some of the important features.
- **5TWSm.02** Use models, including diagrams, to represent and describe scientific phenomena and ideas.

Background information

The aim of page 42 of the *Learner's Book* is to give learners the opportunity to be creative in science and imagine that they have discovered a new type of animal. They apply their learning about adaptation to describe the habitat, what the animal eats and its adaptations. Animals have been chosen because it provides a context for a range of adaptations to be explored by learners. It will be important to give learners time to think and discuss their ideas with others, creativity needs time. This activity also requires learners to apply learning so that information tallies, for example, if it is a predator, then adaptations should enhance its ability to hunt.

Starter activity suggestions

- Show learners photographs of animals that have recently been discovered, such as the Zospeum tholussum snail, a transparent snail. They might not realise that new species of plants and animals are discovered every year.
- Give learners page 27 of the *Workbook* to plan out their new animal.

Activity notes and answers

Page 42 Discovering a new animal
Activity 1
As learners work, check that they are bringing together their learning, encourage them to go back through the *Learner's Book* to remind themselves of the different adaptations they have learnt about. Ask learners to share their initial ideas with a partner who will ask questions to check their science and that adaptations match, for example habitat, prey, predator.

Activity 2
Once their new animal has been designed, learners will create a model of their animal which they could paint (for example, if camouflage is one of the adaptations) and a fact card. You might want to share some Latin names of animals so that learners know what they look and sound like. The models and fact cards could be displayed somewhere prominent in the school for others to view.

Page 43 What have you learnt about adaptation?
Activity 1

a Thick fur coat to stay warm; broad feet so it does not sink into the snow; small ears to reduce heat loss.
b The coat is white in winter to camouflage it against the snow, and darker in the summer to camouflage it against rocks and vegetation.

Activity 2

Rainforest plants	B	C	E
Desert plants	A	D	F

Further activities

- Invite other classes to view the display of 'newly discovered animals' and give learners the chance to talk about the animal they have discovered to other learners.
- Create a big book or display of animals and plants that have been discovered in the last decade. Ask learners to add information to the pictures.

Assessment ideas

- Use the Flashcards and Audio recordings (boost-learning.com) to assess that learners know and understand the new words and concepts covered in this unit.
- Ask learners to complete the checklist on page 43 of the *Learner's Book*, and the self-check activity on page 28 of the *Workbook*.

Success criteria

While completing the activities, assess and record learners.

Learning objectives	Success criteria
5Be.01 Describe how plants and animals are adapted to environments that are hot, cold, wet and/or dry.	Learners design a new animal that has specific adaptations.
5Be.03 Describe the common adaptations of predator and prey animals.	Learners design a new animal that has specific adaptations.
5TWSm.01 Know that a model presents an object, process or idea in a way that shows some of the important features.	Learners use a model of their animal to illustrate adaptation.
5TWSm.02 Use models, including diagrams, to represent and describe scientific phenomena and ideas.	Learners use a model of their animal to illustrate adaptation.

Unit 4 The digestive system

Review of prior learning

Learning objectives from Stages 1–4	LB pages	WB pages	TG pages
3Bs.03 *Identify some of the important organs in humans (limited to brain, heart, stomach, intestine and lungs) and describe their functions.*	44–47	29–30	66–68

Learning objectives overview

Biology	Online resources	LB pages	WB pages	TG pages
Structure and function	Flashcards/Audio			
5Bs.04 Describe the human digestive system, including the functions of the organs involved (limited to mouth, oesophagus, stomach, small intestine, large intestine and anus), and know that many vertebrates have a similar digestive system.	Unit 4 Slides 1–4 Worksheet 8	44–47, 48–50	29–30, 31	66–68, 69–71
Life processes				
5Bp.01 Know that animals, including humans, need an adequate, balanced diet in order to be healthy.	Unit 4 Slides 5–7 Worksheet 9, 10	51–52, 53–54	32–33, 34	71–73, 73–75

Thinking and Working Scientifically	LB pages	WB pages	TG pages
Models and representations			
5TWSm.01 Know that a model presents an object, process or idea in a way that shows some of the important features.	48–49, Activity 1 50, Activity 1		69–71
5TWSm.02 Use models, including diagrams, to represent and describe scientific phenomena and ideas.	48–49, Activity 1 50, Activity 1	31	69–71
Carrying out scientific enquiry			
5TWSc.07 Use a range of secondary information sources to research and select relevant evidence to answer questions.	47, Activity 2–4		66–68
Analysis, evaluation and conclusions			
5TWSa.05 Present and interpret results using tables, bar charts, dot plots and line graphs.	53–54	34	73–75

Science in Context	LB pages	WB pages	TG pages
5SIC.04 Identify people who use science, including professionally, in their area and describe how they use science.	55		76

These learning objectives are reproduced from the Cambridge Primary Science curriculum framework (0097) from 2020. This Cambridge International copyright material is reproduced under licence and remains the intellectual property of Cambridge Assessment International Education.

Cross-curricular links	LB pages	WB pages	TG pages
Mathematics	54, Activity 1	34	74, 75
English	55, Let's talk		76
Global Perspectives® Challenge: How can we stay healthy?	52, Activity 1		72

Focus on the digestive system

Learner's Book
pages 44–47

Workbook pages 29–30

Unit 4 Slides 1–2
Unit 4 Flashcards
Visuals 16–17

Unit 4 Audio

> ### Learning objectives
>
> *Revision of:*
>
> - **3Bs.03** *Identify some of the important organs in humans (limited to brain, heart, stomach, intestine and lungs) and describe their functions.*
> - **5Bs.04** Describe the human digestive system, including the functions of the organs involved (limited to mouth, oesophagus, stomach, small intestine, large intestine and anus), and know that many vertebrates have a similar digestive system.
> - **5TWSc.07** Use a range of secondary information sources to research and select relevant evidence to answer questions.

Background information

The aim of page 44 of the *Learner's Book* is to revisit what learners know from Stage 3 about the organs that make up the digestive system. On page 45, learners are introduced to the digestive system, beginning with a simplified version in the example of a caterpillar. They are asked as a group to create a body outline onto which they place what they already know. This will provide a formative assessment point so that you can identify where they are in their learning and if they hold any misconceptions.

The aim of the activities on pages 46 and 47 is to describe how the digestive system works. The process begins in the mouth where teeth break food down into small pieces and mix it with saliva. The food is then soft enough to swallow. From the mouth, the food moves down the oesophagus, to the stomach where acid helps to break it down further and kill any harmful microorganisms. Here enzymes help to further break down the food before it enters the intestines.

There are two parts to the intestines, the small and large intestine. The small intestine is where the nutrients from the digested food are absorbed into the bloodstream through the walls of the small intestine and carried around the body. Finally, any waste goes into the large intestine where the body gets rid of it as faeces through the anus.

Starter activity suggestions

- Go through the questions on page 44 of the *Learner's Book*, collect answers from the class and ask them to share any additional knowledge about the digestive system. This could be collected as a list of ideas or a mind map displayed on the whiteboard or a working wall. As learners progress through the unit, get them to add new ideas and change any that they subsequently realise were not correct.
- Use Unit 4 Slide 2 (boost-learning.com) as a prompt to help learners think about what happens to food when eaten.

Unit 4 Slide 2 answers

The digestive system

1 a For example: It is parts of the body that work together to take the nutrients from the food and liquids we eat to send around the body.

  b Eating is one of the life processes. If humans and other animals did not eat they would die.

  c Mouth, oesophagus, stomach, small and large intestine.

2 a The teeth grind it into small pieces and saliva softens it so that it can be swallowed.

  b Accept learners' answers – check for misconceptions.

  c Listen to learners' discussions – check for misconceptions.

Activity notes and answers

Page 44 Digestive system quiz
Activity 1

1 a Human mouth: A – canine; B – premolars; C – incisors; D – molars
Lion's mouth: A – incisors; B – canine; C – premolars; D – molars

b Incisor – to cut food; Canine – to tear food; Molars and Premolars – to grind food

c Stomach

d Mixes it and breaks it down

e The small intestine absorbs and moves the nutrients to where they are needed in the body. The large intestine changes waste into faeces.

Activity 2

a–c Listen to learners' responses and use as formative assessment.

Page 45 Digestion
Let's talk

a and **b** Listen to learners' responses and use as formative assessment.

Activity 1

a–c Check learners' drawings. Ask them to explain what they have drawn and written to elicit their prior understanding. Note any misconceptions and acknowledge what they already know.

d Give learners time to discuss their drawings and learn from each other. Listen to their conversations and use as formative assessment.

Pages 46 and 47 The human digestive system
Activity 1

Check learners' drawings and their captions. This provides an opportunity for formative assessment to see what learners already know and also to check for misconceptions. For example, some learners think that there are two tubes in the digestive system, one for food and one for drink.

Activity 2

a The food is mixed and broken down by stomach acid. The acid is important because it further breaks down the food and kills bad microorganisms. The partly digested food then moves to the intestines.

b Check learners' drawings and their captions.

Activity 3

a Nutrients are taken from the digested food and passed through the wall of the small intestine into the blood that takes the nutrients to different parts of the body.
The large intestine changes what is left as waste into faeces to be sent out of the body when we go to the toilet.
The small intestine is about 7 m long; the large intestine is about 1.5 m long.
Faeces is waste; it is what is left after food has been digested. The anus is the opening that the waste comes out of in the bottom.
Not being able to get rid of waste from the body would make someone very ill.

b Check learners' drawings and their captions.

Activity 4

Animals that have one stomach like humans include horses, rabbits, hamsters, dogs and pigs.

Further activities

- As learners work through this unit. Give them time to add information to their large body diagrams of the digestive system.
- Show video clips of the digestive system to help reinforce learning and embed understanding.
- Ask learners to complete *Workbook* pages 29 and 30.

Assessment ideas

Throughout this section check learners' responses, encouraging them to articulate their ideas so that you can check for misunderstandings.

Workbook answers

Page 29 The digestive system

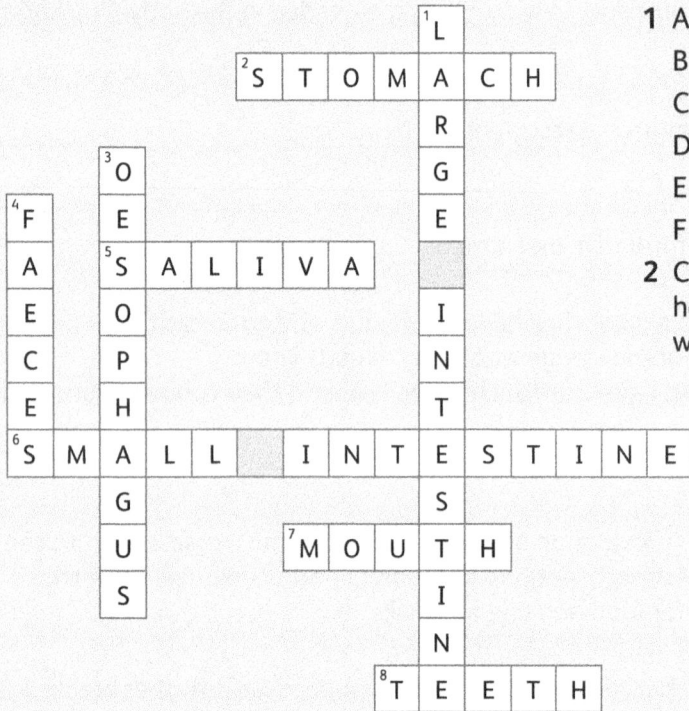

```
                              ¹L
                    ²S  T  O  M  A  C  H
                              R
              ³O              G
    ⁴F        E              E
    A    ⁵S  A  L  I  V  A
    E        O              I
    C        P              N
    E        H              T
   ⁶S  M  A  L  L     I  N  T  E  S  T  I  N  E
    G                       S
    U              ⁷M  O  U  T  H
    S                       I
                            N
                      ⁸T  E  E  T  H
```

Page 30 The digestive system diagram

1 A mouth

   B oesophagus

   C stomach

   D large intestine

   E small intestine

   F anus

2 Check the additional information learners have researched and give them time to share with others in the class.

Success criteria

While completing the activities, assess and record learners.

Learning objectives	Success criteria
3Bs.03 Identify some of the important organs in humans (limited to brain, heart, stomach, intestine and lungs) and describe their functions.	Learners can share what they already know about the digestive system and teeth.
5Bs.04 Describe the human digestive system, including the functions of the organs involved (limited to mouth, oesophagus, stomach, small intestine, large intestine and anus), and know that many vertebrates have a similar digestive system.	Learners can name the main parts of the digestive system and describe what happens. Learners can name two vertebrates with a similar digestive system to humans.
5TWSc.07 Use a range of secondary information sources to research and select relevant evidence to answer questions.	Learners can research new information on the digestive system.

Focus on a model of the digestive system

Learner's Book pages 48–50

Workbook page 31

Worksheet 8

Unit 4 Slides 3–4

Learning objectives

- **5Bs.04** Describe the human digestive system, including the functions of the organs involved (limited to mouth, oesophagus, stomach, small intestine, large intestine and anus), and know that many vertebrates have a similar digestive system.
- **5TWSm.01** Know that a model presents an object, process or idea in a way that shows some of the important features.
- **5TWSm.02** Use models, including diagrams, to represent and describe scientific phenomena and ideas.

Background information

Digestion is a complex process, made all the more challenging for learners because they cannot see the process. For this reason, in science, we use models that replicate systems in a practical way that can help learners to better understand processes such as digestion. Pages 48 and 49 of the *Learner's Book* take learners through a practical activity where they model the digestive system. Prior to beginning the activity discuss the idea of using models in science so that they understand that a model can represent important features and ideas to help us understand parts of science.

On a practical note make sure that they work in small groups so that everyone has a role, learners could video carrying out the activity, explaining as they go along what each part of the model represents; watching it later can help to reinforce learning. The activities on page 50 are designed so that learners apply their knowledge of the digestive system to create their own model.

Starter activity suggestions

- Show learners pictures of different organs of the body. Including the stomach, large and small intestine, lungs, liver, kidney and heart. Ask learners to say which are the odd ones out and why.
- Show learners Unit 4 Slide 3 (boost-learning.com) and discuss the idea of models in science. Use this slide before and after the learners carry out the activities on pages 49–50.
- Show learners Unit 4 Slide 4 (boost-learning.com) to do as a peer-assessment activity.

Unit 4 Slide 3 answers

Modelling the digestive system

Ask and answer before learners make their digestive system model.

a A model in science is a diagram or a physical model of a system or a process.

Ask and answer after learners make their digestive system model.

b–d Learners reflect on how modelling the digestive system helped them to better understand the process, share ideas with the class. Check any areas that learners did not understand so that support can be given.

Unit 4 Slide 4 answers

Digestion

This is a peer-assessment activity that will provide you with the opportunity to listen to responses and formatively assess how well learners understand the process of digestion by applying it to a new context, i.e. a piece of food that they have eaten. Encourage learners to comment and explain to each other why they think their partner's explanation was good or needed, for example, more detail.

Activity notes and answers

Pages 48 and 49 A model of the digestive system
Activity 1
Step 1 – This part represents food being chewed in the mouth.
Step 2 – This is food being digested in the stomach.
Step 3 – Passing from the stomach to the small intestine.
Step 4 – Partly digested food in the small intestine and nutrients passing through the intestine wall into the bloodstream.
Step 5 – Digested food waste in the large intestine and then going to the toilet.

Let's talk
a–c Listen to learners discussing the digestive system model and whether they thought it helped them understand the system any better, and which parts. Ask how the model could be improved.

Challenge yourself!
Ask learners to measure out the large and small intestines using plastic tubing or string, to show how long both are. Learners will realise how much is tucked away in their bodies. They could also measure out other animals' intestines, which will amaze them.

Page 50 Different ideas about the digestive system
Activity 1
a–d Check that learners' models are accurate with correct captions and spelling. Give learners time to storyboard their video clip before they film to ensure that their explanation is accurate. Give learners time to show their models to others and to comment on each other's work.

Further activities

- Learners could repeat the activity to create a teaching video modelling the digestive system to show other learners. They should script the video clip prior to repeating the activity, and check that they have used appropriate scientific language.
- Give learners Worksheet 8 (boost-learning.com) to complete to check that they can apply their knowledge from modelling the digestive system.
- Ask learners to complete *Workbook* page 31.

ICT links

Learners create a video clip of the digestive system model.

Assessment ideas

Use the video clip learners make as a formative assessment and as a peer assessment activity. Ask learners to share their video with other groups and comment on each other's work.

Workbook answers

Page 31 Modelling the digestive system
a Food enters the stomach.
b Drink enters the stomach.
c Food is being digested in the stomach.
d Partly digested food in the small intestine and nutrients passing through the intestine wall into the bloodstream.
e Digested food waste in large intestine and then going to the toilet.

Success criteria

While completing the activities, assess and record learners.

Learning objectives	Success criteria
5Bs.04 Describe the human digestive system, including the functions of the organs involved (limited to mouth, oesophagus, stomach, small intestine, large intestine and anus), and know that many vertebrates have a similar digestive system.	Learners can describe the process of digestion using the correct names of organs involved.
5TWSm.01 Know that a model presents an object, process or idea in a way that shows some of the important features.	Learners can model the digestive system and be able to explain that it is a way of showing how the system works.
5TWSm.02 Use models, including diagrams, to represent and describe scientific phenomena and ideas.	Learners can model the digestive system and be able to explain that it is a way of showing how the system works.

Focus on balanced diets

Learner's Book
pages 51–52

Workbook pages 32–33

Worksheet 9

Unit 4 Slides 5–7
Visuals 18–19

Learning objective

- **5Bp.01** Know that animals, including humans, need an adequate, balanced diet in order to be healthy.

Background information

Humans cannot make their own food, they need to eat to survive and they need food to provide the minerals, proteins, vitamins and fats that help the body to function well. A balanced diet is one where humans eat food from each of the five food groups. These are carbohydrates (starchy foods, such as bread, rice, pasta and potatoes), fruit and vegetables that provide vitamins and fibre, protein from eggs, meat, beans and fish and smaller amounts of food that contain fat. Food containing sugar should be eaten as a treat, not as a regular part of a balanced diet.

The World Health Organisation now classifies obesity as a world-wide problem. The consequences to a person's health of obesity include heart problems, diabetes, osteo arthritis and some cancers. Eating a balanced diet plus exercise can reduce levels of obesity and the associated health problems.

The aim of pages 51 and 52 of the *Learner's Book* is to introduce learners to the idea of the 'balanced food plate', which is an approach that helps to identify the different food groups and which foods to eat more than others.

Starter activity suggestions

- Start the session with an imaginary scenario where the government has told parents and carers that children must be allowed to eat whatever they want to. Ask learners to think about PMIs, what would the Positives, Minuses or Interesting be about doing this. Collect their responses on, for example, a working wall.

- Learners could begin to keep a food diary that can be used to discuss which food groups they are eating from and look at activities such as food swaps later in the unit.

- Celebrate foods from around the world, this could be trying different fruits or small helpings of food from a different country.

- Show learners Unit 4 Slide 5 (boost-learning.com) to elicit what they know about healthy eating; you could come back to this slide at the end of the unit to see if learners' ideas have moved on.

- Show learners Unit 4 Slide 6 (boost-learning.com) and discuss the questions.

> **Unit 4 Slide 6 answers**
>
> **What do you think?**
>
> A = False   B = True   C = True
> D = False   E = True   F = False

Activity notes and answers

Pages 51 and 52 Thinking about balanced diets
Activity 1

1 fruit and vegetables: **D** These foods are full of vitamins and fibre. They help to keep the digestive system healthy and help us to digest our food.
2 carbohydrates: **B** These foods give us energy.
3 protein: **A** These foods help our bodies to grow and repair themselves.
4 dairy foods: **E** These foods are needed for healthy bones and teeth.
5 fats: **C** These foods help us store energy in our bodies.
6 foods high in fats and sugars: **F** These foods should be eaten occasionally, as a treat. It is important not to eat too many foods from this group.

> **Global Perspectives® Challenge**
>
> **How can we stay healthy?**
> Why are fruit and vegetables important in our diet?
>
> **Activity 1** Ask learners to research the benefits of eating fruit and vegetables.
>
> Ask learners to keep a fruit and vegetable food diary to keep track of how much they eat each day.

Activity 2

a and b Accept learners' responses. These will be particular to the individual but check that learners know which group each food belongs to.

c Be careful not to comment on the food they are eating but encourage learners to reflect on alternatives.

d Learners should use the balanced food plate to inform their choices.

e Check that unless the first plate was very well balanced, learners made appropriate choices for alternatives. Ask them to explain why they made those choices.

Activity 3

You could use Unit 4 Slide 7 (boost-learning.com) to support discussion about creating a healthy choice menu for a restaurant or school cafeteria.

a and b Before learners complete their menu, they should explain their draft menu to another group. They should then act on feedback the group gives them about how balanced their menu is and what changes might improve it.

Further activities

- If you have a school canteen, let learners visit the cooks and interview them to find out how they plan balanced meals and food choices for learners. Alternatively, they can visit a local café and discuss their menu. You could ask the owner to challenge the class to create a new, balanced menu for the café.
- Ask learners to complete *Workbook* pages 32 and 33.
- Give learners Worksheet 9 (boost-learning.com) to use during the activities for balanced meals.

Workbook answers

Page 32 The balanced food plate

1 Check learners' drawings.

2 Clockwise the labels are: carbohydrates, proteins, high in fats and sugars, dairy, fresh fruit and vegetables

3 a Accept appropriate responses. Ideally food from each group but in proportion, except foods high in sugar. The body needs food from each group to stay healthy, hence the term balanced.
  b Foods high in sugars, they can lead to tooth decay, diabetes and obesity.

Page 33 Tips for a healthy diet

1 a False   b True   c True   d False   e True

2 Accept appropriate responses that indicate learners understand the food groups and a balanced diet, check by asking learners to explain their choices.

Success criteria

While completing the activities, assess and record learners.

Learning objectives	Success criteria
5Bp.01 Know that animals, including humans, need an adequate, balanced diet in order to be healthy.	Learners can explain why humans need to eat a balanced diet and can name foods that belong to the different food groups.

Focus on making food choices and hidden sugars

Learner's Book
pages 53–54

Workbook page 34

Unit 4 Flashcards
Visual 20

Unit 4 Audio

Learning objectives

- **5Bp.01** Know that animals, including humans, need an adequate, balanced diet in order to be healthy.
- **5TWSa.05** Present and interpret results using tables, bar charts, dot plots and line graphs.

Background information

The aim of pages 53 and 54 of the *Learner's Book* is to raise learners' awareness of the amount of sugar in different foods and that it is easy to consume more than the recommended daily amount, which for children is 24 g. An area to be aware of is that the labels on food are often misleading, they do not always mention sugar but contain ingredients known as hidden sugars, which end in 'ose' such as sucrose, fructose, glucose, others include honey, corn sweetener and molasses. Hence it is easy to consume too much sugar because of the food labelling system.

Learners are often shocked when they weigh out the amount of sugar in, for example, a can of cola. The activities repeatedly return learners to the idea that too much sugar in their diet can lead to diseases such as Type 2 diabetes, as well as tooth decay and obesity. Developing learners' understanding of hidden sugars can help them to make different choices regarding what they eat, although it is important to be sensitive in terms of what is eaten in the home and pressures from peers.

Starter activity suggestions

- Give learners food packaging. Ask them to look for the word 'sugar' or alternative names, and sort food into high, medium and low sugar content.
- Ask learners to discuss what has surprised them from looking at food labels. What have they found out and how could it help them in choosing which foods to eat as part of their balanced diet?

Activity notes and answers

Page 53 Making food choices
Activity 1

a This is not a balanced lunchbox, there are too many foods from the high in fats and sugars group.

b Suggested responses in the table below:

Food	Which food group does it belong to?	Keep or swap
Cola	*foods high in fats and sugars*	*swap for water*
Chocolate	foods high in fats and sugars	swap for a piece of cheese or vegetable sticks
White bread jam sandwich	carbohydrates foods high in fats and sugars	swap for brown or wholemeal bread/pita bread with meat or cheese or salad filling
Crisps	foods high in fats (and salt)	swap for low-fat crisps
Apple	fruit and vegetables	keep

Activity 2

a–c Check individual responses, encouraging learners to choose foods from all food groups except those high in fats and sugars.

Page 54 Hidden sugar dangers
Activity 1

This activity creates cross-curricular links to addition in Mathematics.

a Monday 54 g; Tuesday 72 g; Wednesday 47 g; Thursday 108 g; Friday 69 g; Saturday 72 g; Sunday 82g

b 504 g

c Yes, because the recommended daily amount is 24 g, which would be 168 g per week.

d Sweets

e Yoghurt, it only has 3 g sugar and kiwi fruit that only has 6 g sugar.

f Too much sugar can cause tooth decay, diabetes, obesity.

Further activities

- Learners could keep a diary of the sugar content of food they eat for a week and then plan how they could reduce their intake.
- Learners could use what they have learnt to create an advertising poster to encourage other learners in the school to reduce their sugar intake.
- Learners could apply their learning and produce a leaflet to be sent home to raise awareness of hidden sugars in different foods, suggesting alternatives.
- Ask learners to complete *Workbook* page 34.

ICT links

Learners can use the internet to research Type 2 diabetes.

Assessment ideas

Give each group a card or a piece of paper on which they write five questions related to what has been learnt in this unit, they must use different questions stems, for example: why, what, how, what if, which. They pass their questions to another group who answer them and then pass them back to be marked.

Workbook answers

Page 34 How much sugar?
This activity creates cross-curricular links to addition in the Mathematics curriculum.

1	1 day	24	72	48
	1 week	168	504	336
	1 month (31 days)	744	2 232	1 488
	1 year	8 928	26 784	17 856

2 Type 2 diabetes, tooth decay, obesity

3 a 276 g
   b They would be drinking more than the recommended amount each day, which could lead to health problems, including tooth decay.
   c water, diluted sugar-free fruit juices

Success criteria

While completing the activities, assess and record learners.

Learning objectives	Success criteria
5Bp.01 Know that animals, including humans, need an adequate, balanced diet in order to be healthy.	Learners can explain the effects of too much sugar in their diet and how it can lead to health problems.
5TWSa.05 Present and interpret results using tables, bar charts, dot plots and line graphs.	Learners can interpret results in a table.

Focus on food science

📄 Learner's Book
pages 55–56

✏️ Workbook page 35

⏻ Unit 4 Flashcards

🎧 Unit 4 Audio

Learning objective

- **5SIC.04** Identify people who use science, including professionally, in their area and describe how they use science.

Background information

Page 55 of the *Learner's Book* is a *Science in context* activity where learners are introduced to food scientists as part of the development of their understanding of people who use science in their area of work. Learners may not realise that the many foods they eat are a result of food scientists carrying out a range of research, testing ideas into new foods, ensuring that the nutritional content of food is appropriate and making sure that the food people eat is safe and healthy. It is important that learners appreciate how the science that they learn is applied to different situations by a range of people.

Starter activity suggestions

Ask learners to discuss in their groups what they think a food scientist does, what they might look like, where they think they work and what science they would need for their job. Share ideas across the class, you could even ask learners to draw a food scientist and display their pictures, which might provide some interesting insight into learners thinking.

📄 Activity notes and answers

Page 55 Science in context: Food scientists

✏️ **Let's talk**

This activity creates cross-curricular links to debate, using persuasive language and expressing feelings and opinions, which are covered in English and ESL.

a Accept individual responses.

b For example, balanced diet, the digestive system, different food groups.

c Accept individual responses.

d Listen to how learners use persuasive language to convince their partner to change their mind.

Page 56 What have you learnt about the digestive system?

1 a False   b True   c False   d False

2 Example answer: In the small intestine, nutrients are passed into the bloodstream and taken around the body. In the large intestine, the waste from digestion is made into faeces.

3 Check that learners' choices are appropriate.

4 a Check that learners suggest suitable alternatives, for example low-fat crisps, fruit, yoghurt, water.
  b For example, too much sugar can cause tooth decay or diabetes.

Further activities

Challenge learners to design a new food or crop to solve a world problem, for example obesity, locust plagues or droughts.

ICT links

Learners could use the internet to further research food scientists – they could do this as a home/school activity.

Assessment ideas

- Use the 3, 2, 1 countdown. Ask learners to think of 3 things that they did not know before this topic, 2 things that really surprised them and 1 thing that they have learnt that they are going to use in their daily life from now.
- Use the Flashcards and Audio recordings (boost-learning.com) to assess that learners know and understand the new words and concepts covered in this unit.
- Ask learners to complete the checklist on page 56 of the *Learner's Book*, and the self-check activity on page 35 of the *Workbook*.

Success criteria

While completing the activities, assess and record learners.

Learning objectives	Success criteria
5SIC.04 Identify people who use science, including professionally, in their area and describe how they use science.	Learners can explain what a food scientist does, how they use their scientific knowledge and how their work benefits people.

Unit 5 States of matter

Review of prior learning

Learning objectives from Stages 1–4	LB pages	WB pages	TG pages
4Cp.01 Use the particle model to explain the properties of solids and liquids.	57		79–82

Learning objectives overview

Chemistry	Online resources	LB pages	WB pages	TG pages
Materials and their structure	Flashcards/Audio			
5Cm.01 Use the particle model to describe solid, liquids (including solutions) and gases.	Unit 5 Slide 2	57–59	36–37	79–82
5Cm.02 Understand that substances can be gaseous and know the common gases at room temperature (limited to oxygen, carbon dioxide, water (vapour), nitrogen and hydrogen).		57–59	38	79–82
Properties of materials				
5Cp.01 Know that the ability of a solid to dissolve and the ability of a liquid to act as a solvent are properties of the solid and liquid.	Worksheet 10	66–68		89–91
5Cp.02 Know the main properties of water (limited to boiling point, melting point, expands when it solidifies, and its ability to dissolve a range of substances) and know that water acts differently from many other substances.	Unit 5 Slides 3–6 Unit 5 Video	60–61 62–65	39	82–85, 85–89
Changes to materials				
5Cc.01 Describe the processes of evaporation and condensation, using the particle model and relating the processes to changes in temperature.	Unit 5 Slides 4–5	62–65	40–41	85–89
5Cc.02 Understand that dissolving is a reversible process and investigate how to separate the solvent and solute after a solution is formed.		69–71	43–46	91–94
5Cc.03 Investigate and describe the process of dissolving, and relate it to mixing.	Unit 5 Slide 6	66–68		89–91

Thinking and Working Scientifically	LB pages	WB pages	TG pages
Models and representations			
5TWSm.02 Use models, including diagrams, to represent and describe scientific phenomena and ideas.	58, Activity 2 64, Activity 1–3	39	79–82, 82–85, 85–89
Purpose and planning			
5TWSp.02 Know the features of the five main types of scientific enquiry.	60, Activity 1		82–85
5TWSp.03 Make predictions, referring to relevant scientific knowledge and understanding within familiar and unfamiliar contexts.	60, Activity 2 61, Activity 1 63, Activity 1 64, Activity 1–3 68, Activity 1	39, 43–44	82–85, 85–89, 89–91, 91–94
5TWSp.04 Plan fair test investigations, identifying the independent, dependent and control variables.	61, Activity 2 64, Activity 3 68, Activity 3	39	82–85, 85–89, 89–91

Carrying out scientific enquiry			
5TWSc.03 Choose equipment to carry out an investigation and use it appropriately.	68, Activity 1		89–91
5TWSc.04 Decide when observations and measurements need to be repeated to give more reliable data.	68, Activity 3	44	89–91, 91–94
Analysis, evaluation and conclusions			
5TWSa.01 Describe the accuracy of predictions, based on results.	61, Activity 1 63, Activity 1		82–85, 85–89
5TWSa.03 Make a conclusion from results informed by scientific understanding.	61, Activity 2 63, Activity 1 68, Activity 4	44	82–85, 85–89, 89–91, 91–94
5TWSa.04 Suggest how an investigation could be improved and explain any proposed changes.	68, Activity 4		89–91
5TWSa.05 Present and interpret results using tables, bar charts, dot plots and line graphs.	60, Activity 3		82–85

Science in Context	LB pages	WB pages	TG pages
5SIC.03 Use science to support points when discussing issues, situations or actions.	59		81

These learning objectives are reproduced from the Cambridge Primary Science curriculum framework (0097) from 2020. This Cambridge International copyright material is reproduced under licence and remains the intellectual property of Cambridge Assessment International Education.

Cross-curricular links	LB pages	WB pages	TG pages
Mathematics	60, Activity 3		83
English	63, Activity 2 67, Activity 1		87 90

Focus on solids, liquids and gases

Learner's Book pages 57–59

Workbook pages 36–38

Unit 5 Slides 1–2
Unit 5 Flashcards
Visual 21

Unit 5 Audio

Learning objectives

Revision of:

- **4Cp.01** *Use the particle model to explain the properties of solids and liquids.*
- **5Cm.01** Use the particle model to describe solids, liquids (including solutions) and gases.
- **5Cm.02** Understand that substances can be gaseous and know the common gases at room temperature (limited to oxygen, carbon dioxide, water (vapour), nitrogen and hydrogen).
- **5TWSm.02** Use models, including diagrams, to represent and describe scientific phenomena and ideas.
- **5SIC.03** Use science to support points when discussing issues, situations or actions.

Background information

The purpose of the activities on page 57 of the *Learner's Book* is to recap learning about states of matter (solids, liquids and gases) from Stage 4 and to begin to explore some of the properties of solids.

Page 58 extends learners understanding by introducing the particle theory relating to gas. Remind learners that diagrams are models and help to explain things that we cannot see. Matter is anything that takes up space and has mass.

The states of matter are the distinct forms that matter takes. Four states of matter are observable in everyday life: solid, liquid, gas and plasma. Stage 5 learners only need to know about the first three.

All matter is made up of particles. In a solid, the particles are packed closely together in a rigid structure, so a solid has a fixed shape and volume. In a liquid, the particles are close together, but they can move past one another. Therefore, liquid has a fixed volume, but it does not have a fixed shape; it takes the shape of any container it is poured into. In a gas, the particles are widely spaced and can move about freely. Gas has neither a fixed volume nor a fixed shape, so a gas expands to fill any container. A gas can also be compressed (squashed to fit into a smaller space). Page 59 is a *Science in context* activity that illustrates the use of common gases in different contexts.

Starter activity suggestions

- Give each group objects that include: can of fizzy drink, inflated and not inflated balloons, a range of solids, bottle or cup of water. Ask them to sort them into solids and liquids first, then re-sort them into solids, liquids and gases.
- Display Unit 5 Slide 2 (boost-learning.com). Ask learners to answer the first question and then move on to find out if they can answer the second question.

Unit 5 Slide 2 answers

Solids and liquids

1 a A is a solid because the particles are close together.

  b B is a liquid because the particles are not as close together; they can move past each other.

2 Picture C shows gas because the particles are further apart and can move around easily.

Activity notes and answers

Page 57 Solids, liquids and gases
Activity 1

a Accept reasonable answers. *Solids*: wood, plastic, stone. *Liquids*: water, oil, fizzy drinks.

b Listen to learners' discussions to check their understanding.

Activity 2

Property	Solid	Liquid
keeps its volume	✓	✗
keeps its shape	✓	✗
can be poured	✗	✓
keeps its mass	✗	✗

Activity 3

a and b Check learners' diagrams.

c Let learners self-assess, and check their comments.

Page 58 Gases
Activity 1

Observe learners modelling solids, liquids and gases through role play. Check that they understand the properties of each state. Listen to their discussions. Can they recognise similarities and differences? Are they able to peer assess each other and apply their knowledge of particles and solids, liquids and gases to decide if another group's model is correct?

Activity 2

a–d Accept reasonable models. Learners should show a solid as the group huddled together with no gaps between them, a liquid as some gaps where they are able to move around, and a gas where they can take up space wherever they want to. Learners compare their model with another group and comment on the other group's model to reinforce learning.

Page 59 Science in context: Common gases all around us

Learners are introduced to different gases and how they are used in a range of contexts. Ask learners to create a fact file card to remind them of the name and use of the different gases. Learners should learn how to spell each one.

Further activities

- Get learners to test each other on naming and spelling the common gases: hydrogen, oxygen, nitrogen and carbon dioxide.
- Ask learners to complete *Workbook* pages 36–38.

Home/school activity

Challenge learners to create a list of solids, liquids and gases that they find at home or on the way to and from school. Display these either on a working wall or they could stick their lists in their book.

Assessment ideas

Ask learners (individually or in pairs) to begin a mind map showing what they know about states of matter. If learners work in pairs, ask each learner to write in a different colour so that you can identify each contribution. Then, as learners work through this unit, ask them to add to it on a regular basis.

Workbook answers

Page 36 States of matter

1 a Everything you see around you is <u>matter</u>.
   b All matter weighs something (has <u>mass</u>).
   c All matter takes up space (has <u>volume</u>).
   d Matter exists in one of three <u>states</u>.
   e <u>Solids</u> have a fixed shape and can be held.
   f <u>Liquids</u> feel wet, can be poured and take the shape of their container.
   g <u>Gases</u> move around, fill up spaces and are usually invisible.

2 a Solids: ice, unmelted chocolate, paper wrapper.
      Liquids: cola, melted chocolate.
      Gases: carbon dioxide.
   b Check learners' answers.

Page 37 Particles in solids, liquids and gases

1 a Check learners' diagrams.
   b Example answers:
      This is a solid because the particles are close together and fixed and do not move.
      This is a liquid because the particles are close together but they can move.
      This is a gas because the particles are further apart and can move freely.

Page 38 Gas facts

1 a nitrous oxide   b nitrogen   c propane   d carbon dioxide   e argon
2 Check learners' questions and answers.

While completing the activities, assess and record learners.

Learning objectives	Success criteria
4Cp.01 *Use the particle model to explain the properties of solids and liquids.*	Learners draw diagrams using the particle model to explain the properties of solids and liquids.
5Cm.01 Use the particle model to describe solid, liquids (including solutions) and gases.	Learners can draw diagrams using the particle model to explain the properties of solids, liquids and gases.
5Cm.02 Understand that substances can be gaseous and know the common gases at room temperature (limited to oxygen, carbon dioxide, water (vapour), nitrogen and hydrogen).	Learners can name substances that are common gases (at room temperature).
5TWSm.02 Use models, including diagrams, to represent and describe scientific phenomena and ideas.	Learners can talk about how diagrams represent how the particles are organised in solids, liquids and gases.
5SIC.03 Use science to support points when discussing issues, situations or actions.	Learners can name the common gases and what they are used for.

Focus on water

Learner's Book
pages 60–61

Workbook page 39

Unit 5 Slide 3
Visual 22
Unit 5 Video

Learning objectives

- **5Cp.02** Know the main properties of water (limited to boiling point, melting point, expands when it solidifies, and its ability to dissolve a range of substances) and know that water acts differently from many other substances.
- **5TWSp.02** Know the features of the five main types of scientific enquiry.
- **5TWSp.03** Make predictions, referring to relevant scientific knowledge and understanding within familiar and unfamiliar contexts.
- **5TWSp.04** Plan fair test investigations, identifying the independent, dependent and control variables.
- **5TWSa.01** Describe the accuracy of predictions, based on results.
- **5TWSa.03** Make a conclusion from results informed by scientific understanding.
- **5TWSa.05** Present and interpret results using tables, bar charts, dot plots and line graphs.
- **5TWSm.02** Use models, including diagrams, to represent and describe scientific phenomena and ideas.

Background information

The activities on pages 60 and 61 of the *Learner's Book* focus on the properties of water relating to melting and freezing. If a liquid is cooled sufficiently, it changes state and becomes solid. This process is called freezing (also known as solidification). The temperature at which a liquid freezes or melts is called its freezing/melting point. Different liquids have different freezing points. Water freezes at 0 °C, a number that learners should remember.

Usually, when things freeze, they shrink, so they are smaller. In water this does not happen, this is due to the arrangement of the water molecules, which instead of moving closer together take up more space and so the ice expands. This is very easy to show: place water in a plastic bottle, mark where the water level is, place it in the freezer and observe the difference between the level of the water (liquid) and the water as a solid (ice). This also means that ice is less dense, which is why it floats in water.

Starter activity suggestions

- Using a mini whiteboard, ask pairs to draft and redraft definitions for freezing and melting. Ask them to swap with another pair and peer assess their definitions, adding comments or suggesting corrections.
- Discuss page 60 with learners, ask them to talk in their group and work out how Class 5 carried out the activity in preparation for carrying out the same activity. Get each group to map out their fair test on a large sheet of paper and then each group visit another group and carry out a peer-assessment on their plan, leaving two comments, one positive and one saying what they might improve on.
- After learners have completed page 61, show Unit 5 Slide 3 (boost-learning.com) and discuss the answers. Ask learners to draw their diagram on a mini-whiteboard, then hold it up so that you can formatively assess if learners have understood what happens when water freezes. Remind learners that their diagrams model a scientific idea.

Unit 5 Slide 3 answers

Water freezing

a liquid to solid

b 0 °C

c

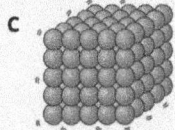

Activity notes and answers

Page 60 Properties of water
Activity 1
a Fair test because they changed the type of liquids, kept the amounts of liquid the same, and measured the time it took each liquid to freeze.
b They placed the same amount of different liquids into the spaces in an ice cube tray and put it in the freezer for a set amount of time, observing every 15 minutes to see what was happening to each liquid.
c Change in colour, texture, whether it expanded or shrank.
d Accept reasonable answers. Yes, but some learners might suggest that this should be repeated with three trays of ice cubes to see if the same thing happened to each one.

Activity 2

a–c Learners carry out the test (one ice cube tray per group of four learners). Ask them to write down their predictions and check that they know how to collect and record data.

Activity 3
This activity creates cross-curricular links to bar charts in Mathematics.
a Learners should observe that the water expanded when frozen.
b Learners should be able to check their predictions and decide, not that they were 100 % accurate, but whether their predictions were similar to their results.
c Check that learners know which data to put on the x and y-axis, and what the intervals should be for the scale on the y-axis.
d Accept reasonable responses.

Page 61 What happens when water freezes?
Activity 1

a Ask learners to explain why they have been asked to mark the level of the water and take a photograph before putting the cup of water in the freezer (for before and after comparisons).

b If learners' predictions are not appropriate, do not change them at this point. Their learning will be more effective if they are challenged by a result they had not predicted.

c–f Ask learners to discuss their observations of the water before and after and which predictions they made that were correct and if there were any changes they did not predict. Listen to their conversations, asking questions to clarify learning. For example, liquid water solidifies, expands, has bubbles, goes cloudy.

Activity 2

a–d Learners repeat the previous test but choose different liquids. In terms of practicality, it is better if each group chooses a different liquid, so that only one liquid from each group needs to be frozen. For this activity, learners should apply what they have learnt so far about how different liquids freeze when they predict what will happen in this activity. The reason for a report no longer than 75 words is to help develop learners' ability to write in a concise way, using correct scientific vocabulary. Their report should include their conclusion that water is different because it expands when it freezes.

> ## Further activities
>
> - Learners could repeat the activities from this section at home, using different safe liquids that are available.
> - Watch the Unit 5 Video: Frost/ice forming on glass (boost-learning.com). Discuss what learners observe happening.
> - Ask learners to complete *Workbook* page 39.

> ## Workbook answers
>
> **Page 39 Investigating freezing**
>
> **a** and **b** Check learners' plans for the investigation. Ensure that learners have given a clear prediction and drawn a labelled diagram showing what they plan to do in their investigation. They should say what they will observe or measure, and how they will make sure that these observations or measurements are reliable. Learners should also identify any potential problems, and explain how these could be avoided.
>
> **c** Water is different. When it freezes, the <u>particles</u> link together in a way that means there are <u>spaces</u> between them. This means they take up even more <u>space</u> as a solid than they do as a liquid. Water <u>expands</u> when it freezes. Instead of getting smaller when it freezes, water gets <u>bigger</u>.
>
> **d** Normal solid: A; Frozen state: B

> ## Success criteria
>
> While completing the activities, assess and record learners.
>
> | Learning objectives | Success criteria |
> | --- | --- |
> | **5Cp.02** Know the main properties of water (limited to boiling point, melting point, expands when it solidifies, and its ability to dissolve a range of substances) and know that water acts differently from many other substances. | Learners can describe that water freezes (solidifies) at 0°C and expands when it freezes. |
> | **5TWSp.02** Know the features of the five main types of scientific enquiry. | Learners can identify a fair test scientific enquiry. |

Learning objectives	Success criteria
5TWSp.03 Make predictions, referring to relevant scientific knowledge and understanding within familiar and unfamiliar contexts.	Learners can make predictions about what will happen to different liquids including water when they are frozen.
5TWSp.04 Plan fair test investigations, identifying the independent, dependent and control variables.	Learners can plan and carry out a fair test investigation.
5TWSa.01 Describe the accuracy of predictions, based on results.	Learners can describe the accuracy of their predictions.
5TWSa.03 Make a conclusion from results informed by scientific understanding.	Learners can use their results from a fair test investigation to draw appropriate conclusions.
5TWSa.05 Present and interpret results using tables, bar charts, dot plots and line graphs.	Learners can present results as a bar chart.
5TWSm.02 Use models, including diagrams, to represent and describe scientific phenomena and ideas.	Learners can say that a diagram of particles of solids, liquids and gases models scientific ideas.

Focus on evaporation and condensation

Learner's Book
pages 62–65

Workbook pages 40–42

Unit 5 Slides 4–5
Visuals 23–24

Learning objectives

- **5Cp.02** Know the main properties of water (limited to boiling point, melting point, expands when it solidifies, and its ability to dissolve a range of substances) and know that water acts differently from many other substances.
- **5Cc.01** Describe the processes of evaporation and condensation, using the particle model and relating the processes to changes in temperature.
- **5TWSp.03** Make predictions, referring to relevant scientific knowledge and understanding within familiar and unfamiliar contexts.
- **5TWSp.04** Plan fair test investigations, identifying the independent, dependent and control variables.
- **5TWSa.01** Describe the accuracy of predictions, based on results.
- **5TWSa.03** Make a conclusion from results informed by scientific understanding.
- **5TWSm.02** Use models, including diagrams, to represent and describe scientific phenomena and ideas.

Background information

The purpose of page 62 of the *Learner's Book* is to develop learners' understanding of what happens when water boils. The temperature at which a liquid boils is called its boiling point. The boiling point of freshwater (at sea level) is 100 °C. If a liquid continues to be heated after boiling, the temperature does not rise beyond its boiling point, so the temperature of boiling water does not rise beyond 100 °C.

When a liquid is heated to a high enough temperature, it boils. When a liquid boils, it turns to gas throughout its volume, not just on the surface. This is why there are bubbles in a boiling liquid: they are made of the gas the liquid has turned into. Learners often think that the steam they see rising from boiling water is water vapour. It is not. Water vapour is invisible. Steam is made up of tiny droplets of water, which form when water vapour rising from the boiling water meets cooler air; some of it condenses (changes state) back into water.

The activities on pages 63 and 64 focus on evaporation, which is the process in which a liquid changes state to become a gas. Evaporation takes place only at the surface of a liquid and at all temperatures. But as the temperature increases, so does the rate of evaporation.

On page 65, learners develop their understanding of the process of condensation that happens when a gas is cooled enough to turn into a liquid. Typically, this happens when a gas comes into contact with a cool surface. The greater the difference between the temperature of the gas and the temperature of the surface it comes into contact with, the greater the rate of condensation.

Starter activity suggestions

- Give learners a short quiz on what they have learnt so far in this unit. This will help to consolidate their ideas and give them the opportunity to use the correct scientific language. You could divide the class into teams, get them to identify a scribe to write their answers on a mini-whiteboard. Questions could include:
  - *Name one property of matter.* (It has mass/takes up space/has volume)
  - *Which states of matter have a fixed volume?* (Solids and liquids)
  - *Which states of matter do not have a fixed shape?* (Liquids and gases)
  - *Which state of matter can be compressed?* (Gases)
  - *Why is sand not a liquid?* (Not wet/does not form a puddle/individual sand grains have a fixed shape)
  - *Name three different gases.*
  - *How can you speed up melting?* (Increase temperature)
- Use Unit 5 Slides 4 and 5 (boost-learning.com).

Unit 5 Slide 4 answers

Where has the water gone?

a The water has evaporated into the air.
b Evaporation
c The temperature of the air, whether it is hot or cold.
d Accept, for example the air, clouds

Unit 5 Slide 5 answers

What is happening?

a The air in the bathroom.
b The hot air hit the cold surface of the bathroom mirror.
c Condensation
d For example, on a car window, on the outside of a glass.

Activity notes and answers

Page 62 What happens when water boils?
Let's talk
a–c Demonstrate to small groups or the class what happens when water boils, focusing their attention on the bubbles in the water, indicating that water boils throughout. The slight gap between the water or spout of the kettle, the water vapour (gas), has to rise above the spout until it meets cooler air. Then it condenses into what many learners call steam. Use this section as an opportunity to impress upon learners the health and safety issues relating to being around boiling water.

Let's talk

a Learners' responses. For example: boiling a kettle.

b Boiling water can burn or scald you as it is very hot. Boiling water must be handled with care.

c Boiling water can burn or scald you.

Page 63 Evaporation

Let's talk

This is an opportunity to challenge learners to make sense of evaporation using the particle model. As the water in the puddle is heated, the particles move around more, and the ones at the surface move into the surrounding air.

Activity 1

a–d Learners should be able predict that the water will evaporate, and to explain that when the water on the paper towel is heated, the particles begin to move around more and more until they move into the air.

e and **f** The paper towel dries out, as the water has evaporated. Check that their sentences include 'heat', 'particles', 'air', 'evaporate/evaporated'.

Activity 2

The identification of root words creates cross-curricular links to English and ESL.

a and **b** Ask learners to share their hand signals for the word 'evaporate' and how they will remember to spell 'evaporates', 'evaporated' and 'evaporation' using the root word 'evaporate'.

Page 64 Evaporation all around us

Activity 1

a–e Check that learners have set up the activity correctly and are able to explain their prediction, using the particle model. If learners use photographs or videos, they can create a 'before' and 'after' recording with an explanation.

Activity 2

a–e This is similar to the previous activity. The aim is to assess whether learners can apply the concept of evaporation and the particle model in a range of contexts.

Activity 3

a–d Check that learners have measured the liquids and placed containers in the same place, to ensure a fair test. Check their responses, which should explain evaporation using the particle model. They will also probably notice that some liquids take longer to evaporate than others, and that some might leave a residue (you could ask them what this is).

Page 65 Condensation

Activity 1

a Example: mist/water appears on the mirror from breath.

b Example: From my breath, from inside my body.

c Condensation

Activity 2

d Water forming.

e Water vapour has hit the cold cup, cooled and formed water droplets, condensed.

f Water has come from the air, the water vapour cools, the particles move closer together forming liquid.

g and **h** The ice melted, became liquid. The water on the outside of the plastic cup evaporated. The processes are melting and evaporation.

Challenge yourself!

When the horse breathes out, the water vapour in the breath condenses into lots of tiny droplets.

Further activities

- Ask learners to complete *Workbook* pages 40–42.

- Ask learners how they could show that water evaporates from wet things or containers with water; for example, leave items with water around the room or school to evaporate (such as wet paper, water in containers, wet sponges, wet fabrics, wet clothes on a line). Challenge learners to predict how long will it take for the water in each item to evaporate.

- Set a home/school activity where learners look around their home and local environment to find out where water or other liquids have evaporated/could evaporate.
- Challenge learners to find as many single words as they can from evaporation. Who in the class can set the record?

Workbook answers

Page 40 Evaporation

1 a The liquid in the puddle is being <u>heated</u> by the Sun.

 b The particles have more energy so they move into the <u>air</u>.

 c When this happens, the particles of water change state from a <u>liquid</u> to a <u>gas</u>.

 d This process is called <u>evaporation</u>.

2 Example answer: When a liquid changes to a gas, it is called evaporation.

 Examples of evaporation: clothes on a washing line; wet floor drying; drying hair with a hairdryer; water evaporating from a puddle; evaporating salt water to leave salt; sweat from our bodies evaporating.

3 Check learners' diagrams.

Page 41 Boiling and condensation

1 a Heat the water to 100 °C.

 b Water vapour

 c Tiny droplets of water – condensed water

 d 100 °C

 e No

2 a Condensation happens when a **gas** is cooled and changes state into a **liquid**.

 b water

 c Example: water condensed from the air

 d Example: in a steamy bathroom on a cold bathroom mirror

Page 42 Change of state clues

1 a heating **b** melting
 c cooling **d** boiling
 e freezing **f** evaporation

2 a–e Check learners' definitions/clues. Their partner could also carry out a peer assessment using the dictionary at the back of the *Learner's Book*.

Success criteria

While completing the activities, assess and record learners.

Learning objectives	Success criteria
5Cp.02 Know the main properties of water (limited to boiling point, melting point, expands when it solidifies, and its ability to dissolve a range of substances) and know that water acts differently from many other substances.	Learners can describe what happens when water boils, and say it boils at 100 °C.
5Cc.01 Describe the processes of evaporation and condensation, using the particle model and relating the processes to changes in temperature.	Learners can use the particle model to describe what happens and why water evaporates.
5TWSp.03 Make predictions, referring to relevant scientific knowledge and understanding within familiar and unfamiliar contexts.	Learners can make predictions about what will happen when liquid evaporates.

Learning objectives	Success criteria
5TWSp.04 Plan fair test investigations, identifying the independent, dependent and control variables.	Learners can plan and carry out a fair test investigation.
5TWSa.01 Describe the accuracy of predictions, based on results.	Learners can describe the accuracy of their predictions.
5TWSa.03 Make a conclusion from results informed by scientific understanding.	Learners can use their results from a fair test investigation to draw appropriate conclusions.
5TWSm.02 Use models, including diagrams, to represent and describe scientific phenomena and ideas.	Learners can say that a diagram of particles of solids, liquids and gases models scientific ideas.

Focus on dissolving

Learner's Book
pages 66–68

Worksheet 10

Unit 5 Slide 6

Learning objectives

- **5Cp.01** Know that the ability of a solid to dissolve and the ability of a liquid to act as a solvent are properties of the solid and liquid.
- **5Cc.03** Investigate and describe the process of dissolving, and relate it to mixing.
- **5TWSp.03** Make predictions, referring to relevant scientific knowledge and understanding within familiar and unfamiliar contexts.
- **5TWSc.03** Choose equipment to carry out an investigation and use it appropriately.
- **5TWSc.04** Decide when observations and measurements need to be repeated to give more reliable data.
- **5TWSa.03** Make a conclusion from results informed by scientific understanding.
- **5TWSa.04** Suggest how an investigation could be improved and explain any proposed changes.

Background information

The activities on page 66 of the *Learner's Book* recap learners' understanding of mixtures, as a precursor to developing learners' understanding that a solution is a mixture. The aim of pages 67 and 68 is to build on learning about dissolving.

A 'solution' is a mixture of one or more substances, the 'solute' is the substance dissolved in another substance, which is called the 'solvent'. Solutions can be made up of substances in any of the states of matter, but the most familiar are solid in liquid (such as salt dissolved in water), gas in liquid (such as air dissolved in water) and gas in gas (for example, air is a solution of oxygen and other gases dissolved in nitrogen). At this stage, learners only need to know about solutions of solids in liquids. When a solid dissolves in a liquid, the particles of the solute cannot be seen by the naked eye. The solution looks clear. When a solid is mixed with a liquid but does not dissolve in it, it forms a different kind of mixture called a 'suspension'. A suspension is cloudy.

Starter activity suggestions

- Before the lesson, prepare three identical glasses. Fill one with a salt solution, one with a sugar solution and one with water to which you have added a colourless flavouring (such as peppermint oil). Display the three glasses at the front of the class. Ask learners: *What is in the glasses?* Ask a volunteer to come up and take a 1 ml measuring spoonful from a glass, taste it and then describe the taste. Stress the importance of tasting such a small amount of liquid from the glass (salt solutions are not safe to drink). Repeat for the other two glasses with a different volunteer each time. Recap the term 'dissolve'. Establish that something has been dissolved in the water in each glass that has changed its taste. Ask learners to guess what these might be.

- At the end of the activities on pages 66–68 of the *Learner's Book*, show learners Unit 5 Slide 6 (boost-learning.com).

Unit 5 Slide 6 answers

Dissolving – what do you know?

1 a Dissolved sugar in the water   **b** Water   **c** Sugar
2 It would be cloudy.
3 Soluble means the substance can be dissolved in a liquid.
   Insoluble means the substance cannot be dissolved in a liquid.
4 Reversible change

Activity notes and answers

Page 66 Mixtures
Let's talk
a Example: using a magnet, picking them out by hand.
b Sieve flour from rice.
c Examples: Sweets, chopped vegetables in salad.

Let's talk
Example answer: Pour the water through a sieve into another jar so the pebbles stay in the sieve, pick the pebbles out of the jar.
Separate soil from water using a filter, for example filter paper, cloth.

Page 67 Dissolving
Activity 1
This activity links to English and ESL. Give learners time to plan and make their own mini word cards. Remind learners to use their cards to make sure that they use correct scientific vocabulary.

Page 68 Investigating solutions
Activity 1
a–d Check learners' results. Discuss the results with the class, and which substances surprised them (perhaps the flour that does not dissolve in water but forms a suspension).

Activity 2
a salt, sugar
b–c Questions could include temperature, number of stirs, amount of solute, amount of water.

Activity 3
Learners should plan their fair test. This does not have to be a lengthy piece of writing; they could use notes, a map of their ideas or pictures so that the majority of the time is spent on carrying out their test and analysing their results. Discuss the idea of repeat measurements and taking averages to verify (check) their results, so that they can have confidence in them.

Activity 4
a–d Accept reasonable answers, making sure that learners use their data to justify conclusions.

Further activities

- **Home/school activity** Challenge learners to carry out tests at home (with permission) to find out which safe kitchen ingredients dissolve in water, and share their results with the class, including photographs or video clips.
- Give learners Worksheet 10 (boost-learning.com) to use to carry out a test to find out how the temperature of water affects the time taken for sugar to dissolve.

Assessment ideas

Ask learners to tell their partner what they know about dissolving. They should ask their partner if they have missed an idea or a word and then explain it.

Success criteria

While completing the activities, assess and record learners.

Learning objectives	Success criteria
5Cp.01 Know that the ability of a solid to dissolve and the ability of a liquid to act as a solvent are properties of the solid and liquid.	Learners can understand the properties of solids and liquids.
5Cc.03 Investigate and describe the process of dissolving, and relate it to mixing.	Learners can describe the process of dissolving and say that it is a mixture.
5TWSp.03 Make predictions, referring to relevant scientific knowledge and understanding within familiar and unfamiliar contexts.	Learners can make predictions about which substance is soluble and which is insoluble.
5TWSc.03 Choose equipment to carry out an investigation and use it appropriately.	Learners can carry out an investigation choosing and using appropriate equipment.
5TWSc.04 Decide when observations and measurements need to be repeated to give more reliable data.	Learners observe results and can explain why they have taken repeat measurements.
5TWSa.03 Make a conclusion from results informed by scientific understanding.	Learners can use their scientific knowledge about dissolving to draw conclusions.
5TWSa.04 Suggest how an investigation could be improved and explain any proposed changes.	Learners can make suggestions about how to improve their investigation.

Focus on dissolving as a reversible process

Learner's Book pages 69–72

Workbook pages 43–46

Unit 5 Flashcards Visual 25

Unit 5 Audio

Learning objectives

- **5Cc.02** Understand that dissolving is a reversible process and investigate how to separate the solvent and solute after a solution is formed.
- **5TWSp.03** Make predictions, referring to relevant scientific knowledge and understanding within familiar and unfamiliar contexts.
- **5TWSc.04** Decide when observations and measurements need to be repeated to give more reliable data.
- **5TWSa.03** Make a conclusion from results informed by scientific understanding.

Background information

Learners already know that some mixtures are easy to separate, pages 69–71 of the *Learner's Book* develop learners' understanding of separating mixtures through filtration and evaporation.

Salt is soluble in water. It dissolves to form a solution. Sand, on the other hand, does not dissolve in water. It is insoluble, but it is easy to separate by filtering the mixture. Salt can be separated from a solution through evaporation. This solution is left where the water can evaporate and the salt remains.

On pages 70 and 71, learners create coloured sugar crystals. While these take up to a week to form, learners get excited watching them slowly develop, so do leave time for this activity.

Starter activity suggestions

Give each group different kinds of mixtures, for example dry mixtures, soluble and insoluble materials in water, ask them to describe the mixtures and how the contents of each one can be separated. Listen to responses, challenging them to use correct scientific vocabulary. Use this as a formative assessment opportunity to find out how confident they are and what they understand about separating mixtures. Decide whether some learners need additional learning opportunities to master the key ideas.

Activity notes and answers

Page 69 Dissolving is a reversible process: filtration
Activity 1

1 a Learners should be able to label each mixture as a solution or suspension. This will depend on if they observe particles of the solid floating in the water after stirring the mixture thoroughly.

b and **c** Learners should observe that when they pour a suspension through the filter, particles of the solid are left behind on the filter paper. They should observe that when they pour a solution through the filter, there are no particles left behind.

d–h Learners carry out the rest of the activity. They should note that the suspensions can be separated through filtering but the solutions cannot.

Let's talk

a Learners should be able to state that solutions could not be separated by putting them through a filter.

b This is because, in a solution, the particles of the solid have combined with the particles of the liquid to form a single substance.

Page 70 Dissolving is a reversible process: evaporation
Let's talk

a Example: Place the solution in a container without a lid or saucer and leave it somewhere warm.

b The water.

c The salt.

Activity 1

a–d Learners should note that the water evaporates and leaves the solid (solute) from each solution on each saucer.

e The solution, which is a mixture that has been separated using evaporation.

Let's talk

Listen to conversations. Which learners are confident in their answers? Which learners are struggling to apply the idea of evaporation?

Pages 71 and 72 How did it work?
Activity 1

Prior to carrying out this activity, ask learners to read the instructions, then explain what they have to do to their partner. For this activity to work, learners need to know what to do in advance and to follow the instructions step by step. Once complete, the solution must be left untouched for about a week.

Work safely ⚠️

This activity requires an adult to boil water.

If the intention is for learners to create a video report of this activity, then it is useful for learners to work in groups of three or four, so that two learners can carry out the activity. One learner videos and the other is the narrator explaining each step as it happens. They should use correct scientific vocabulary, including 'boil', 'solute', 'solvent', 'solution'. It is useful for the group to have a 'pretend' run through carrying out the actions with the script before doing it for real.

Activity 2

a and **b** Give learners an audience for their video report, either others in their own or another class, or post videos on the school website.

Page 73 What have you learnt about states of matter?
Activity 1

Property	Solid	Liquid	Gas
keeps its volume	✓	✗	✗
keeps its shape	✓	✗	✗
can be poured	✗	✓	✗
keeps its mass	✗	✗	✗
act as a solvent	✗	✓	✗
act as a solute	✓	✗	✗

Activity 2
A Condensation   **B** Evaporation   **C** Condensation   **D** Evaporation

Activity 3
A Solvent   **2** The liquid into which a solid has been dissolved.
B Solution   **1** A mixture of a solid and a liquid that looks clear.

ICT links

Learners create a video report of their activity.

Further activities

- Ask learners to complete *Workbook* pages 43–45.
- Ask learners to use their research skills to find out how sea salt is produced by evaporating seawater.

Workbook answers

Page 43 Dissolving and solutions

1		Soluble materials	Insoluble materials
	what they do when mixed with water	dissolve	do not dissolve
	what the mixture looks like	clear	cloudy
	what the mixture is called	solution	suspension
	how to separate the mixture	evaporation	filtering

2 a Example: salt, sugar, coffee   **b** Example: sand, soil, pasta, flour   **c** Suspension
   d Solution   **e i** The water will evaporate   **ii** The solute – sugar

Page 44 Stir it up

1 Accept reasonable answers. Stirring sugar (a solute) into a solvent (water) speeds up the rate of dissolving because it helps distribute the solute (sugar) particles throughout the solvent (water).

2 a Use the same amount of water for each cup, use the same amount of sugar, stir for the same amount of time.

b Repeat readings and take an average, this helps to see if the readings for each sugar solution are roughly the same, if not, then a reading can be taken again.

3 a Example: Yes because they repeated their readings. No, they should have taken five readings, or they could have tested different sugars as well.

b The answer will be individual to the learner, check their answers.

Page 45 Word search

D	I	S	S	O	L	V	E	A	E
I	C	X	C	V	B	B	R	S	V
S	O	L	U	T	I	O	N	Q	A
S	N	G	H	J	K	I	L	Z	P
O	D	F	V	C	X	L	B	X	O
L	E	Q	R	D	C	I	M	C	R
V	N	W	V	E	D	N	F	N	A
I	S	E	R	Y	E	G	H	J	T
N	A	R	U	H	E	Z	U	K	I
G	T	T	O	B	D	H	E	L	O
M	I	Y	P	S	W	J	M	P	N
J	O	U	A	Q	W	A	B	O	I
U	N	I	V	E	R	T	T	J	T
Q	W	E	R	T	Y	U	G	E	Y
B	O	I	L	V	B	N	M	H	R

Assessment ideas

- Use the Flashcards and Audio recordings (boost-learning.com) to assess that learners know and understand the new words and concepts covered in this unit.
- Ask learners to complete the checklist on page 73 of the *Learner's Book*, and the self-check activity on page 46 of the *Workbook*.

Success criteria

While completing the activities, assess and record learners.

Learning objectives	Success criteria
5Cc.02 Understand that dissolving is a reversible process and investigate how to separate the solvent and solute after a solution is formed.	Learners can reverse dissolving by separating solvent and solute through evaporation.
5TWSp.03 Make predictions, referring to relevant scientific knowledge and understanding within familiar and unfamiliar contexts.	Learners can explain their predictions using knowledge about dissolving.
5TWSc.04 Decide when observations and measurements need to be repeated to give more reliable data.	Learners can explain why repeat readings give more reliable data.
5TWSa.03 Make a conclusion from results informed by scientific understanding.	Learners can use scientific understanding about dissolving and evaporation to inform conclusions.

Unit 6 Forces

Review of prior learning

Learning objectives from Stages 1–4	LB pages	WB pages	TG pages
3Pf.02 *Know that gravity on Earth is a force that pulls towards the centre of the Earth.*	83–85		104–108
3Pf.03 *Know that friction is a force created between surfaces when they move against each other and it makes this movement harder.*	80–82		101–104
3Pf.04 *Describe how smooth and rough surfaces can generate different amounts of friction.*	80–82		101–104

Learning objectives overview

Physics	Online resources	LB pages	WB pages	TG pages
Forces and energy	Flashcards/Audio			
5Pf.01 Identify a range of forces (limited to gravity, applied forces, normal forces, upthrust, friction, air resistance and water resistance).	Unit 6 Slides 2, 4–7	74–77, 80–82, 83–85, 86–88	48	96–98, 101–104, 104–108, 108–112
5Pf.02 Know that an object may have multiple forces acting upon it, even when at rest.		74–77, 78–79		96–98, 99–100
5Pf.03 Use force diagrams to show the name and direction of forces acting on an object.	Unit 6 Slide 3	78–79, 83–85, 86–88	47	99–100, 104–108, 108–112

Thinking and Working Scientifically	LB pages	WB pages	TG pages
Models and representations			
5TWSm.02 Use models, including diagrams, to represent and describe scientific phenomena and ideas.	74, Activity 1 78, Activity 1		96–98, 98–100
Purpose and planning			
5TWSp.03 Make predictions, referring to relevant scientific knowledge and understanding within familiar and unfamiliar contexts.	74, Activity 2 80, Activity 1 81, Activity 1		96–98, 101–104
5TWSp.04 Plan fair test investigations, identifying the independent, dependent and control variables.	82, Activity 2 84, Activity 3		101–104, 104–108
Carrying out scientific enquiry			
5TWSc.01 Sort, group and classify objects, materials and living things through testing, observation and using secondary information.	74, Activity 2 82, Activity 1		96–98, 100–102
5TWSc.04 Decide when observations and measurements need to be repeated to give more reliable data.	82, Activity 2 84, Activity 2 85, Activity 1 87, Activity 1	51	101–104, 104–108, 108–112
5TWSc.05 Take appropriately accurate measurements.	84, Activity 2		104–108
5TWSc.06 Carry out practical work safely.	87, Activity 1		108–112
5TWSc.08 Collect and record observations and/or measurements in tables and diagrams appropriate to the type of scientific enquiry.	75, Activity 4 81, Activity 1 85, Activity 2 86, Activity 1	52	96–98, 101–104, 104–108, 108–112
Analysis, evaluation and conclusions			
5TWSa.02 Describe patterns in results, including identifying any anomalous results.	85, Activity 1 87, Activity 2	51, 52	104–108, 108–112

5TWSa.03 Make a conclusion from results informed by scientific understanding.	82, Activity 3 85, Activity 1 87, Activity 2	52	101–104, 104– 108, 108–112
5TWSa.04 Suggest how an investigation could be improved and explain any proposed changes.	82, Activity 2		101–104
5TWSa.05 Present and interpret results using tables, bar charts, dot plots and line graphs.	82, Activity 3 86, Activity 2 87, Activity 2	52	101–104, 108–112

Science in Context	LB pages	WB pages	TG pages
5SIC.03 Use science to support points when discussing issues, situations or actions.	88		110

These learning objectives are reproduced from the Cambridge Primary Science curriculum framework (0097) from 2020. This Cambridge International copyright material is reproduced under licence and remains the intellectual property of Cambridge Assessment International Education.

Cross-curricular links	LB pages	WB pages	TG pages
Mathematics	80, Activity 3 82, Activity 3 85, Activity 1 86, Activity 2 87, Activity 2	50, 51	102 106 107 109 110

Focus on applied and normal forces

Learner's Book
pages 74–77

Unit 6 Slides 1–2
Unit 6 Flashcards
Visual 26

Unit 6 Audio

Learning objectives

- **5Pf.01** Identify a range of forces (limited to gravity, applied forces, normal forces, upthrust, friction, air resistance and water resistance).
- **5Pf.02** Know that an object may have multiple forces acting upon it, even when at rest.
- **5TWSm.02** Use models, including diagrams, to represent and describe scientific phenomena and ideas.
- **5TWSc.01** Sort, group and classify objects, materials and living things through testing, observation and using secondary information.
- **5TWSc.08** Collect and record observations and/or measurements in tables and diagrams appropriate to the type of scientific enquiry.
- **5TWSp.03** Make predictions, referring to relevant scientific knowledge and understanding within familiar and unfamiliar contexts.

Background information

The aim of page 74 of the *Learner's Book* is to find out what learners remember from previous work on forces through carrying out a set of interactive practical activities.

The focus of pages 75 and 76 is to introduce two new scientific terms relating to forces; an 'applied force' and a 'normal force'. An applied force is applied to an object by a person or another object. For example, if a child pushes their chair under the table, they are applying a force on the chair, an applied force. A normal force (also called a support force) supports the weight of an object on a surface, such as a child sitting on a chair. It acts in the opposite direction of gravity, exerting an upward force.

These are not easy concepts for learners, and they might need lots of practical experience in the classroom and outdoors to help them remember these two forces.

Starter activity suggestions

- Show learners Unit 6 Slide 2 (boost-learning.com), use this as a quick quiz where each group writes their answers on an individual whiteboard and then after a set time, say 2 minutes, the class stops and the groups swap their answers for another group to mark.
- Start this topic with a Physical Education lesson where learners revise pushes, pulls, twists, stretching, squashing as well as discussing friction, for example shoes, ropes, mats.

Unit 6 Slide 2 answers

Quick quiz

Accept reasonable answers from learners. Encourage them to use words such as 'push', 'pull', 'slide', 'stretch', 'squash', 'friction', 'slippery', 'force', 'direction'.

Activity notes and answers

Pages 74 and 75 Forces
Activity 1
a–b Give learners time to make and play the table football game, remind them to take a photograph for their book and think about the forces in action as they play.

c Learners should be able to explain that:
- They push air through the straw, which then pushes the ball and makes it move.
- The bigger the force, the farther and faster it will move the object; the smaller the force, the slower the object will move, and the less distance the object will cover.
- To change the direction of the ball, the straw must be moved so that the force of the moving air can push it in that direction.
It would be harder to play on the rough surface of the grass because there is more friction.

Activity 2
a–c Check that learners sorted the objects into three groups: *floats*, *sinks* and *don't know*. They must then test their predictions and record their results, including whether the *don't know* objects (which they were unsure about) sank or floated. Remind them to take a photograph and write down three things about floating and sinking.

Activity 3
a–b Learners should be able to describe that the scrunched-up paper falls quickly to the ground; the flat sheet floats and takes longer. Gravity was acting on both pieces of paper.

Activity 4
a–c Check that learners measure correctly, using the newton meter. They should record their results in table format and work out the averages. Identify the object that took the biggest force to move, noting that it was the biggest/heaviest.

Page 76 Learning about applied forces
Let's talk
A The child is applying an applied force – pulling to make the toy move.
B The person is using an applied force – pushing the car to make it move.
C The child is applying an applied force – pushing to make the ball move.
D The bird is using an applied force – pulling the worm to make it move.

Activity 1
a–c Check learners' drawings and labels.

Page 77 Learning about normal forces
Let's talk
Listen to learners' discussions. They should be able to talk about the table pushing up and supporting the book, and gravity pulling the book downwards towards the Earth. They should be able to say that the table supporting the book is a normal force.

Activity 1

Check learners' responses; these could include learners sitting on a chair, a table standing on the floor, objects on a table. The object holding each one up is exerting a normal force on the object. Check that learners realise that more than one force is acting on the object, for example normal force and gravity.

Further activities

Take learners outdoors into the school grounds or local park to identify and photograph applied and normal forces. Photographs can be stuck in their books and annotated.

Assessment ideas

Give learners time to 'mark' each other's books, leaving comments on what is good and what could be improved directly onto their pages on or sticky notes.

Success criteria

While completing the activities, assess and record learners.

Learning objectives	Success criteria
5Pf.01 Identify a range of forces (limited to gravity, applied forces, normal forces, upthrust, friction, air resistance and water resistance).	Learners can identify where normal forces are in action.
5Pf.02 Know that an object may have multiple forces acting upon it, even when at rest.	Learners can identify where more than one force is acting on an object.
5TWSm.02 Use models, including diagrams, to represent and describe scientific phenomena and ideas.	Learners can use a model to represent forces.
5TWSc.01 Sort, group and classify objects, materials and living things through testing, observation and using secondary information.	Learners can sort objects into groups that float or sink.
5TWSc.08 Collect and record observations and/or measurements in tables and diagrams appropriate to the type of scientific enquiry.	Learners can record their force measurements in a table.
5TWSp.03 Make predictions, referring to relevant scientific knowledge and understanding within familiar and unfamiliar contexts.	Learners can make predictions about objects that float or sink.

Focus on force diagrams

Learner's Book pages 78–79

Workbook page 47

Unit 6 Slide 3
Visuals 27–28

Learning objectives

- **5Pf.02** Know that an object may have multiple forces acting upon it, even when at rest.
- **5Pf.03** Use force diagrams to show the name and direction of forces acting on an object.
- **5TWSm.02** Use models, including diagrams, to represent and describe scientific phenomena and ideas.

Background information

The aim of the activities on pages 78 and 79 of the *Learner's Book* is to develop learners' understanding of force diagrams. A force diagram shows the forces acting on an object, using arrows to show both the direction of the force and how strong the force is. The longer the force arrow, the bigger the force; the shorter the force arrow, the smaller the force. Forces can be challenging concepts for learners as they cannot be seen, and force diagrams show invisible forces. Discuss that scientists often use diagrams to show forces so that other people can understand what is happening.

Starter activity suggestions

- When teaching force diagrams, an important rule is that the arrows must always touch the objects they act on. Give learners arrow cards of different lengths to use on objects on their table, checking that the arrow is positioned correctly. Learners could discuss what each other has done and peer assess.
- Show learners Unit 6 Slide 3 (boost-learning.com).

Unit 6 Slide 3 answers

Force diagrams

Ask volunteers to come up to the board and indicate where force arrows should go from and to:

foot to ball   baseball bat to ball   centre of tennis racket to ball

Activity notes and answers

Page 78 Force diagrams (1)
Activity 1

Picture 1: **A** weight	**B** normal force	Picture 2: **C** weight	**D** normal force
Picture 3: **E** normal force	**F** weight	Picture 4: **G** normal force	**H** weight

Page 79 Force diagrams (2)
Activity 1

Picture 1: **A** applied force	**B** friction	Picture 2: **C** applied force	**D** friction
Picture 3: **E** applied force	**F** friction	Picture 4: **G** applied force	**H** friction

Activity 2

Check that learners' diagrams show the applied force arrow from the child's hand on the string going in the direction of the toy cart, and friction arrows from the wheels in the opposite direction to their movement.

Further activities

- Return learners to the arrow cards. Challenge them to put the arrows around the classroom where they can see normal forces and weight, creating 3D force diagrams.
- Challenge learners to video other children in the playground and add commentary about forces.
- Ask learners to complete *Workbook* page 47.

✏️ **Workbook answers**

Page 47 Force arrows

1 a

b

c

d

2 For example: pushing a door open, pulling on socks.

ICT links

- Learners could find pictures on the internet and place force arrows to show direction and strength of the force.
- Learners use an electronic tablet to video each other playing and creating commentary about forces.

Assessment ideas

Learners find pictures of objects in magazines and draw arrows and write labels to show the forces at work.

Success criteria

While completing the activities, assess and record learners.

Learning objectives	Success criteria
5Pf.02 Know that an object may have multiple forces acting upon it, even when at rest.	Learners can identify where more than one force is acting on an object.
5Pf.03 Use force diagrams to show the name and direction of forces acting on an object.	Learners can read and draw force diagrams showing the name and direction of forces acting on an object.
5TWSm.02 Use models, including diagrams, to represent and describe scientific phenomena and ideas.	Learners can use diagrams to represent scientific ideas.

Focus on friction

Learner's Book
pages 80–82

Workbook page 48

Unit 6 Slide 4

Learning objectives

Revision of:

- **3Pf.03** *Know that friction is a force created between surfaces when they move against each other and it makes this movement harder.*
- **3Pf.04** *Describe how smooth and rough surfaces can generate different amounts of friction.*
- **5Pf.01** Identify a range of forces (limited to gravity, applied forces, normal forces, upthrust, friction, air resistance and water resistance).
- **5TWSp.03** Make predictions, referring to relevant scientific knowledge and understanding within familiar and unfamiliar contexts.
- **5TWSc.01** Sort, group and classify objects, materials and living things through testing, observation and using secondary information.
- **5TWSc.04** Decide when observations and measurements need to be repeated to give more reliable data.
- **5TWSc.08** Collect and record observations and/or measurements in tables and diagrams appropriate to the type of scientific enquiry.
- **5TWSa.03** Make a conclusion from results informed by scientific understanding.
- **5TWSa.04** Suggest how an investigation could be improved and explain any proposed changes.
- **5TWSa.05** Present and interpret results using tables, bar charts, dot plots and line graphs.

Background information

The purpose of the activities on pages 80–82 of the *Learner's Book* is for learners to practise a range of scientific enquiry skills in the context of investigating friction.

Some surfaces produce more friction than others. In general, the smoother and/or harder the surface, the less friction it produces; the rougher and/or softer the surface, the more friction it produces.

The more friction a surface produces, the more it opposes the motion of an object in contact with it. This means it will take more force to start a stationary object sliding or rolling along a high friction surface than along a low friction surface. This also means that an object sliding or rolling freely over a high friction surface will move more slowly.

Starter activity suggestions

Bring in a range of materials and objects and ask learners to sort them into high friction and low friction, that is those with not much friction (smooth) and those with a lot of friction (rough). Give them time to explore moving one surface over the other with combinations of smooth over smooth, rough over rough, smooth over rough and listen to their discussions.

📄 **Activity notes and answers**

Page 80 How friction affects motion
Activity 1
The paper in the books needs to be uncoated for this activity to work. Learners should be unable to pull the books apart. This is due to the force of friction between the pages of the books.

Activity 2
a The roll on the wooden ramp will reach the end of the ramp first.

b Wood, a smooth surface, produces less friction than carpet. Less friction means the roll will slow down less, and so reach the end of the ramp first.

c–e Check that learners do the activity shown in the illustration correctly. The ramps should be of the same length and positioned at the same angle. The only difference between them should be the material covering them (one should be hard and smooth, and the other covered in carpet or another soft, rough material).

Activity 3
This activity creates opportunities for cross-curricular links with Mathematics, where learners are required to use a Carroll diagram.
Lots of friction: useful D; not useful A
Not much friction: useful C; not useful B

Page 81 Investigating friction (1)
Let's talk
Learners should be able to use previous experience to suggest that some surfaces do produce more friction than others. They should be able to explain their thinking, using specific examples.

Activity 1
c Force meter readings are likely to be more accurate if a different person takes them to the person who is pulling the shoe. Remind learners that the reading should be taken when the shoe starts to move (when it overcomes friction), not when the shoe is constantly moving.

d Force meter readings in this test can fluctuate quite a bit, which is why it is a good idea to take multiple readings for each surface and calculate average values.

i Learners should be able to conclude that the smoothest, hardest surfaces create the least friction and the roughest, softest surfaces create the most friction.

Challenge yourself!
a The other forces acting on the shoe were the force of gravity and the reaction force.

b We can ignore the effects of these forces because they were balanced, so they did not affect the motion of the shoe.

Page 82 Investigating friction (2)
Activity 1
Learners should be able to apply what they have already learnt about how a material's properties (roughness/smoothness and hardness/softness) affect the amount of friction it produces and explain their thinking to their partner.

Activity 2
a Learners could ask questions such as: *Does the type of sole affect the amount of force needed to move the shoe? How does the weight in a shoe affect the amount of force needed to move the shoe? Does a slope affect the amount of force needed to move the shoe on each surface?*

b Ask learners to say which force meter they will use and why. Explain why repeat readings are used or not used.

c Tell learners to say what they think is good about their partner's test and why and offer one suggestion for improvement and explain why.

Activity 3
This activity creates opportunities for cross-curricular links with Mathematics, where learners are required to present results in a line graph or bar chart.

a Check that learners have carried out their fair test in an appropriate way.

b Ask learners to look at their table of data and think about the general rule for deciding which type of graph to use: word and number = bar chart; number and number = line graph.

Make sure that learners use their knowledge about friction, data from their test and key scientific vocabulary in their conclusion.

Further activities

- Show learners Unit 6 Slide 4 (boost-learning.com). Collect learners' ideas, for example high friction: brakes, tyres, handle; low friction: chain, saddle. If possible, get learners to bring their bicycle to school so that they can identify friction on their bike. They could take photographs and annotate them.
- Ask learners to complete *Workbook* page 48.

Unit 6 Slide 4 answers

Friction and bikes

For example, high friction is needed on the tread of the wheels to grip the road and the brakes so that the bike can be stopped. Low friction is needed on the cogs so they go round smoothly, and on the wheel axle, so the wheel turns smoothly.

Workbook answers

Page 48 Friction in everyday life

1 Friction is the <u>force</u> between two <u>surfaces</u> that are moving across one another.

   <u>Friction</u> always works in the <u>opposite</u> direction to the direction in which the object is moving.

2 **a** more friction – so tyres grip on uneven or muddy land

   b more friction – so trainers grip the road

   c less friction – so skateboard wheels can move along the surface easily

   d less friction – so that the fidget spinner can go fast

   e more friction – so the rock climber can grip more easily

Assessment ideas

Ask learners to apply their understanding of friction in a different context, for example a bicycle. This provides a good opportunity for formative assessment.

Success criteria

While completing the activities, assess and record learners.

Learning objectives	Success criteria
3Pf.03 Know that friction is a force created between surfaces when they move against each other and it makes this movement harder.	Learners can identify friction between two surfaces and that this can make movement harder.
3Pf.04 Describe how smooth and rough surfaces can generate different amounts of friction.	Learners can identify where rough and smooth surfaces create different amounts of friction.
5Pf.01 Identify a range of forces (limited to gravity, applied forces, normal forces, upthrust, friction, air resistance and water resistance).	Learners can describe friction in a range of contexts.

Learning objectives	Success criteria
5TWSp.03 Make predictions, referring to relevant scientific knowledge and understanding within familiar and unfamiliar contexts.	Learners can make predictions using scientific knowledge about friction.
5TWSc.01 Sort, group and classify objects, materials and living things through testing, observation and using secondary information.	Learners can order materials from least friction to greatest friction.
5TWSc.04 Decide when observations and measurements need to be repeated to give more reliable data.	Learners know when to repeat readings and why.
5TWSc.08 Collect and record observations and/or measurements in tables and diagrams appropriate to the type of scientific enquiry.	Learners can collect measurements and record them in a table.
5TWSa.03 Make a conclusion from results informed by scientific understanding.	Learners can use results to inform their conclusions.
5TWSa.04 Suggest how an investigation could be improved and explain any proposed changes.	Learners can make suggestions on how to improve an investigation.
5TWSa.05 Present and interpret results using tables, bar charts, dot plots and line graphs.	Learners can present results in a bar chart or line graph.

Focus on air resistance

Learner's Book
pages 83–85

Workbook pages 49–51

Worksheet 11

Unit 6 Slide 5
Visuals 29–30

Learning objectives

Revision of:
- *3Pf.02 Know that gravity on Earth is a force that pulls towards the centre of the Earth.*
- **5Pf.01** Identify a range of forces (limited to gravity, applied forces, normal forces, upthrust, friction, air resistance and water resistance).
- **5Pf.03** Use force diagrams to show the name and direction of forces acting on an object.
- **5TWSp.04** Plan fair test investigations, identifying the independent, dependent and control variables.
- **5TWSc.04** Decide when observations and measurements need to be repeated to give more reliable data.
- **5TWSc.05** Take appropriately accurate measurements.
- **5TWSc.08** Collect and record observations and/or measurements in tables and diagrams appropriate to the type of scientific enquiry.
- **5TWSa.02** Describe patterns in results, including identifying any anomalous results.
- **5TWSa.03** Make a conclusion from results informed by scientific understanding.

Background information

The purpose of the activities on pages 83–85 of the *Learner's Book* is for learners to develop their understanding of air resistance. Learners will practise a range of scientific enquiry skills in the context of investigating air resistance.

Air resistance is a kind of friction that occurs between the surface of a falling object and the air around it; it slows down the object. The greater the surface area, the greater the air resistance. Think back to earlier in the unit when learners were asked to compare dropping a scrunched-up sheet of paper and a flat sheet. The scrunched-up one fell faster because there is less air resistance. Parachutes are designed to take advantage of air resistance whereas cars and planes are designed to reduce air resistance.

Starter activity suggestions

- Get learners to repeat earlier activities in this unit where they dropped a scrunched-up paper ball and a flat sheet of paper. Learners share ideas.

- Take learners into the school grounds. Working in pairs with a large piece of card, one learner runs with the card parallel to the side of their body, and then with the card in front of them, comparing what they feel. Both learners compare their results.

Activity notes and answers

Page 83 Air resistance
Let's talk
Gravity and air resistance

Let's talk
The crumpled sheet of paper shows that the force of gravity is greater than air resistance. The flat sheet of paper shows that the force of air resistance is greater than the force of gravity.
Listen to learners' discussions to find out if they understand what the force diagrams are showing.
If learners are unsure, discuss the diagrams either with individuals or as a whole class.

Page 84 Parachutes
Activity 1
a–e Learners follow instructions.

f The parachute canopy opens and it falls slowly to the ground.

g Air resistance is acting on the parachute slowing it down.

h

Activity 2
a–d Learners should find that each reading is different because the reaction time of humans is not fast enough to note start and finish times. This means that the readings are not reliable. So, to get a reading that is roughly around the correct time, repeat readings are used to verify the results, which makes the final reading used more reliable than just using one result.

Activity 3
a–c Questions could include: *How does the material the canopy is made from affect how long it takes the parachute to fall? How does the weight of the person affect how long it takes the parachute to fall? How does the area of the canopy affect how long it takes the parachute to fall?*

Learners choose a question to answer by carrying out a fair test, check that learners use repeat readings and calculate the average. They should then convert their table of results into a bar chart or line graph.

Page 85 Using data

Activity 1

This activity creates cross-curricular links to surface area in Mathematics.

a Area of the parachute.

b Type of material, length of string, size of model person, height of drop.

c Time in seconds.

d To check (verify) numbers range, so that the data is more believable (reliable).

e The bigger the area of the canopy, the longer it takes the parachute to drop/descend.

f Because the bigger the area of the canopy, the more air is underneath and the greater the air resistance.

g Because the smaller the area of the canopy, the less air is underneath. Therefore, the air resistance is less and gravity pulls the parachute down towards the ground.

Activity 2

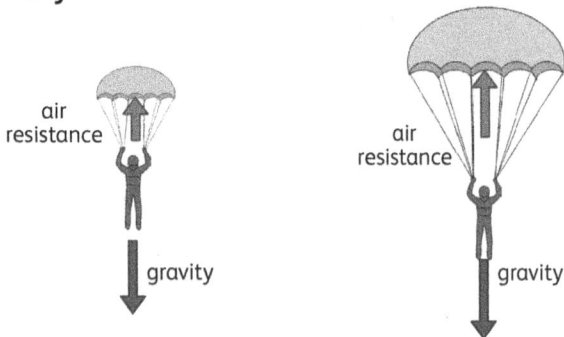

Activity 3

a To slow the jet plane down when it lands.

b The parachute uses air resistance to slow the plane down (this is horizontal rather than vertical as in the parachutes learners have been testing).

c

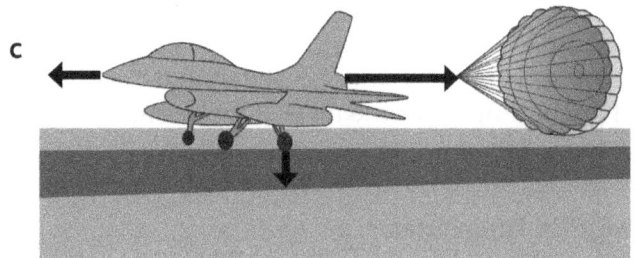

Further activities

- Learners will have answered different questions. Get them to share their data and results and then challenge learners to use the information to make and test a super parachute using the best material, mass of person, area of canopy. Learners share data to see if they have improved on the parachutes they had previously made. Get them to create a force diagram to show forces in action on the parachute.

- Give learners Worksheet 11 (boost-learning.com) to support drawing a bar chart.

- Show learners Unit 6 Slide 5 (boost-learning.com) and challenge them to apply what they know about friction and air resistance to the activity in each photograph.

- Ask learners to complete *Workbook* pages 49–51.

Unit 6 Slide 5 answers

For example:

1 Cyclist – narrow cycle to reduce air resistance, helmet aerodynamic, smooth fabric, tight-fitting clothing so streamlined body, rider makes shape that is streamlined to reduce friction.

2 Skier – smooth fabric, tight fitting clothing so streamlined body. Skis smooth to reduce friction.

3 Parachutist – large canopy to increase air resistance.

4 Skater – smooth fabric, tight fitting clothing so streamlined body, skater makes shape that is streamlined to reduce friction.

ICT links

Learners could video a parachute descent and use the slow-motion facility to observe how it moves.

Assessment ideas

Use graph work to carry out a formative assessment of learners' ability to produce a graph. This will identify areas where individuals or groups require support and further experience.

Workbook answers

Page 49 Air resistance

1 a Lorry A has a flat front and Lorry B is shaped in a curve on the top.
  b Lorry B
  c Lorry B because it is designed to reduce air resistance so the lorry does not have to use more fuel working against air resistance.
  d Less fuel means that the lorry gives out fewer gases (emissions).

2 a Train B is the Japanese bullet train because the front is shaped like a bullet, it reduces friction (it is aerodynamic).
  b The front is shaped like a bullet, it reduces friction (it is aerodynamic).
  c Train B the Japanese bullet train, it is aerodynamic in shape, which means it can travel faster.
  d Train B the Japanese bullet train because it will use less fuel as it is shaped to reduce air resistance.

Page 50 Parachutes (1)

1 Air resistance is a <u>force</u> that acts on an <u>object</u> as it <u>moves</u> through the <u>air</u>.

  <u>Air resistance</u> acts in the <u>opposite</u> direction to the direction an object is moving.

  This means that as a <u>parachute</u> falls to the ground, the air resistance <u>pushes</u> up on the parachute <u>slowing</u> it down.

2 This activity creates a cross-curricular link with Mathematics.
  a Cotton 3.57   Denim 2.38   Nylon 3.88   Plastic bag 5.10
  b Check that learners' bar charts correctly display the data, the *x* and *y* axis are correct and the title is 'This is a bar chart to show which material makes the best parachute.' (Learners should draw a draft of their bar chart in the *Workbook* and redraw a neat version on a sheet of graph paper.)
  c The best material is the plastic bag because it took 5.10 seconds, which was the slowest descent.

Page 51 Parachutes (2)

1 This activity creates a cross-curricular link with Mathematics.
  a 25 cm² – 1.50 seconds   100 cm² – 2.25 seconds   225 cm² – 2.47 seconds
    400 cm² – 4.22 seconds   625 cm² – 5.32 seconds
  b Check learners' line graphs. Make sure they label the *x*-axis and the *y*-axis (check scale used on both axes). Line graph title should be 'This is a graph to show how the area of the canopy affects how long it takes for the parachute to descend.' (Learners should draw a draft of their line graph in the *Workbook* and redraw a neat version on a sheet of graph paper.)

2 a To make their data more reliable.
  b The area of the canopy was increased and the time the parachute took to descend increased, so the parachute with the largest area was the slowest to descend.
  c The greater the area of the parachute, the more air resistance.
  d Check learners' diagrams.

Success criteria

While completing the activities, assess and record learners.

Learning objectives	Success criteria
3Pf.02 Know that gravity on Earth is a force that pulls towards the centre of the Earth.	Learners can identify when gravity is in action on an object.
5Pf.01 Identify a range of forces (limited to gravity, applied forces, normal forces, upthrust, friction, air resistance and water resistance).	Learners can explain air resistance in different contexts.
5Pf.03 Use force diagrams to show the name and direction of forces acting on an object.	Learners draw force diagrams to show direction of forces acting on an object.
5TWSp.04 Plan fair test investigations, identifying the independent, dependent and control variables.	Learners can plan and carry out a fair test to answer a question.
5TWSc.04 Decide when observations and measurements need to be repeated to give more reliable data.	Learners can make repeated readings when timing a parachute descent.
5TWSc.05 Take appropriately accurate measurements.	Learners can use a stopwatch or timing facility on, for example an electronic tablet.
5TWSc.08 Collect and record observations and/or measurements in tables and diagrams appropriate to the type of scientific enquiry.	Learners can record observations using tables and diagrams.
5TWSa.02 Describe patterns in results, including identifying any anomalous results.	Learners can describe the pattern in results.
5TWSa.03 Make a conclusion from results informed by scientific understanding.	Learners can use their results from parachute fair tests and scientific understanding of forces (air resistance and gravity) to draw conclusions.

Focus on upthrust

Learner's Book pages 86–89

Workbook pages 52–53

Worksheet 12

Unit 6 Slides 6–8
Unit 6 Flashcards
Visuals 31–32

Unit 6 Audio

Learning objectives

- **5Pf.01** Identify a range of forces (limited to gravity, applied forces, normal forces, upthrust, friction, air resistance and water resistance).
- **5Pf.03** Use force diagrams to show the name and direction of forces acting on an object.
- **5TWSc.04** Decide when observations and measurements need to be repeated to give more reliable data.
- **5TWSc.05** Take appropriately accurate measurements.
- **5TWSc.06** Carry out practical work safely.
- **5TWSc.08** Collect and record observations and/or measurements in tables and diagrams appropriate to the type of scientific enquiry.
- **5TWSa.03** Make a conclusion from results informed by scientific understanding.

- **5TWSa.05** Present and interpret results using tables, bar charts, dot plots and line graphs.
- **5SIC.03** Use science to support points when discussing issues, situations or actions.

Background information

Learners will have come across the 'feel of upthrust' when they were learning about floating and sinking. The aim of page 86 of the *Learner's Book* is to introduce learners to how we can show that upthrust occurs by using measurements. It is useful to focus on key words, breaking down the word *up* and *thrust*, to help learners understand and remember the word. Upthrust is a force that pushes things up. Objects float in water because of upthrust. Learners can see how the weight of a stone appears to get less when it is immersed in water, this is due to the water pushing up on the stone.

Page 87 focuses on water resistance through engaging learners in a fair test investigation. Here is an opportunity to slow down learning and discuss each aspect of the test with learners to check their understanding. Focus on their thinking to set up the fair test, the link between their prediction and results and their reasoning for trusting (or not) their data; for example, the numbers show an expected pattern, there are no 'unusual' (anomalous) results. By slowing down teaching and learning, you will be able to formatively assess how well they have mastered elements of thinking and working scientifically.

Page 88 challenges learners to apply their knowledge of streamlining in different contexts, once again providing an opportunity for formative assessment to check that learners can apply understanding.

Starter activity suggestions

- Take learners out into the school grounds. Give each group a bowl of water and an inflated balloon. Ask learners to push the balloon into the water and feel the water pushing back on the balloon (upthrust). If they push the balloon down into the water and then let go, they can observe how the balloon 'bounces' back up, this is the force of the water pushing back on the balloon.
- For those learners who need support with creating a bar chart, give them Worksheet 12 (boost-learning.com).

Activity notes and answers

Page 86 Upthrust

Think like a scientist! Note that the force arrows in the diagram go from the centre of the object – discuss this with learners.

Activity 1

a–c Learners should note that their data shows that objects appear to weigh more in the air than in water because of upthrust.

Activity 2

This activity creates opportunities for cross-curricular links with Mathematics, where learners are required to present results in a bar chart.

Check that learners' bar charts have two bars for each object – learners might need support in understanding how to create this chart.

a They should note that out of the water the objects weigh more than in the water.
b The water is pushing up on the object and the scale shows that it weighs less in water.
c Because of upthrust on the object.
d Check that their force arrows are in the correct position (see *Think like a scientist!* diagram).

Page 87 Water resistance

Prior to working on water resistance, show learners Unit 6 Slide 6 (boost-learning.com) to discuss how they can carry out their fair test.

Activity 1

a Example: cube, cone, sphere, rectangular prism.

b Accept their suggestions. Their thinking should be that shapes that are pointed will be more streamlined.

c The 3D shapes

d The amount of material in the shape, amount of water, how it is put into the water.

e Time to reach the bottom of the cylinder.

f Learners will be measuring by sight, which is not reliable, so repeat readings are needed.

g Example: Table

Shape	Reading 1 Time (sec)	Reading 2 Time (sec)	Reading 3 Time (sec)	Average

h If they are carrying this out in the classroom the floor might become slippery with water, so care is needed not to spill water, and to mop up any spills.

Activity 2 This activity creates opportunities for cross-curricular links with bar charts in Mathematics.

a Check that all learners have a role in their group.

b Accept appropriate answers – the usual pattern is that the cone when placed point down into the water is the fastest.

c That shapes that are pointed move through water quicker.

d Listen to learners' discussions.

e Check learners' bar charts to make sure that learners have information on the correct axis and that the y-axis has an appropriate scale.

Page 88 Science in context: Uses of streamlining

Let's talk

The shark has an elongated shape that is long and tapered at each end. This makes it streamlined, which makes it faster in the water to catch prey. The turtle has a body that is thin and flat with a curved shell. That makes it streamlined to move through the water more easily to avoid predators.

Let's talk

The shape of the car is streamlined to look better and more sporty but challenge learners to think about how the streamlined shape affects speed (reduces air resistance so helps to increase speed) and how it uses less fuel.

The cyclist wants to win races, so needs to reduce air resistance that could slow the cyclist down, therefore shape and material of helmet, clothing, how narrow the bike is, all help to reduce friction with the air.

Activity 1

Check learners' research and that they realise that similar shapes are used to reduce friction in both water and the air.

Activity 2

Share and display learners' collages, getting learners to discuss how they show streamlining in air and water. Check that they can explain why.

Page 89 What have you learnt about forces?

Activity 1

gravity – the force that pulls objects towards themselves, for example ball and ground.

normal force – the force that supports the weight of an object on a surface.

applied force – a push or a pull.

air resistance – friction between a moving object and the surrounding air.

water resistance – friction between a moving object and the surrounding water.

upthrust – push of water upwards on an object.

Activity 2

A

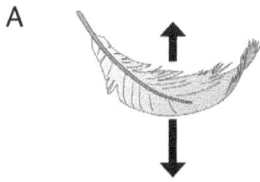

B

Activity 3

The penguin is streamlined so that it can overcome water resistance and move through water easily to avoid predators and catch prey.

Activity 4

Further activities

- Show learners Unit 6 Slides 7 and 8 (boost-learning.com).
- Ask learners to complete *Workbook* page 52.

Unit 6 Slide 7 answers

Using forces

A The swimmer makes a shape that is streamlined to move through water more easily and quickly.

B The boat is a thin shape with a pointed front to move through water more easily and quickly.

C The bird changes its shape to pointed and thin and streamlined to enter the water more easily and move through the water more quickly to catch fish.

Unit 6 Slide 8 answers

Apollo 16 Splashdown

- Parachutes use air resistance to slow the capsule down.
- Upthrust pushes the capsule up in the water – helping it to float.

Workbook answers

Page 52 Weight in water

1 a

Object	A	B	C	D	E	F
Weight in air (N)	25 N	19 N	9 N	10 N	28 N	34 N
Weight in water (N)	5 N	4 N	2 N	3 N	7 N	9 N

  b Check learners' bar charts. (Learners should draw a draft of their bar chart in the *Workbook* and redraw a neat version on a sheet of graph paper.)

2 In the air the objects weigh more than when they are placed in the water.

3 This is because of the upthrust of the water.

ICT links

Learners use the internet to research pictures and use a computer software program to create a collage.

Assessment ideas

- Use the Flashcards and Audio recordings (boost-learning.com) to assess that learners know and understand the new words and concepts covered in this unit.
- Ask learners to complete the checklist on page 88 of the *Learner's Book*, and the self-check activity on page 53 of the *Workbook*.

Success criteria

While completing the activities, assess and record learners.

Learning objectives	Success criteria
5Pf.01 Identify a range of forces (limited to gravity, applied forces, normal forces, upthrust, friction, air resistance and water resistance).	Learners can identify friction, air and water resistance in a range of contexts.
5Pf.03 Use force diagrams to show the name and direction of forces acting on an object.	Learners can draw force diagrams in different contexts.
5TWSc.04 Decide when observations and measurements need to be repeated to give more reliable data.	Learners can use repeat readings and explain why they are using them.
5TWSc.05 Take appropriately accurate measurements.	Learners can take accurate measurements.
5TWSc.06 Carry out practical work safely.	Learners can identify safety issues and manage them to work safely.
5TWSc.08 Collect and record observations and/or measurements in tables and diagrams appropriate to the type of scientific enquiry.	Learners record measurements using a table.
5TWSa.03 Make a conclusion from results informed by scientific understanding.	Learners use data and scientific understanding about forces to draw conclusions.
5TWSa.05 Present and interpret results using tables, bar charts, dot plots and line graphs.	Learners draw bar charts and line graphs and interpret data in each.
5SIC.03 Use science to support points when discussing issues, situations or actions.	Learners can use science to discuss streamlining.

Unit 7 Sound

Review of prior learning

Learning objectives from Stages 1–4	LB pages	WB pages	TG pages
1Ps.01 Identify different sources of sound.	90–94		114–117
1Ps.02 Explore that as sound travels from a source it becomes quieter.	90–94	54, 56	114–117

Learning objectives overview

Physics	Online resources	LB pages	WB pages	TG pages
Light and sound	Flashcards/Audio			
5Ps.01 Investigate how sounds are made by vibrating sources.	Unit 7 Slides 2–4	90–94, 95–96, 97–100, 101–102	55, 60	114–117, 117–119, 119–122 122–126
5Ps.02 Describe sounds in terms of high or low pitch and loud or quiet volume.	Unit 7 Slide 5	95–96, 97–100, 101–102	60	117–119, 119–122, 122–126
5Ps.03 Investigate how to change the volume and pitch of sounds.	Unit 7 Slide 6	97–100, 101–102	59	119–122, 122–126

Thinking and Working Scientifically	LB pages	WB pages	TG pages
Purpose and planning			
5TWSp.03 Make predictions, referring to relevant scientific knowledge and understanding within familiar and unfamiliar contexts.	94, Activity 2 98, Activity 1	55, 58	114–117, 119–122
Carrying out scientific enquiry			
5TWSc.06 Carry out practical work safely.	98, Activity 2		119–122
5TWSc.07 Use a range of secondary information sources to research and select relevant evidence to answer questions.	101, Activity 1		122–126
Analysis, evaluation and conclusions			
5TWSa.01 Describe the accuracy of predictions, based on results.	98, Activity 1		119–122
5TWSa.02 Describe patterns in results, including identifying any anomalous results.	98, Activity 2		119–122
5TWSa.03 Make a conclusion from results informed by scientific understanding.	92, Activity 1–2 93, Activity 1–3 94, Activity 1–2	54–56	114–117
5TWSa.05 Present and interpret results using tables, bar charts, dot plots and line graphs.	90, Activity 4	56	114–117

Science in Context	LB pages	WB pages	TG pages
5SIC.03 Use science to support points when discussing issues, situations or actions.	101		123

These learning objectives are reproduced from the Cambridge Primary Science curriculum framework (0097) from 2020. This Cambridge International copyright material is reproduced under licence and remains the intellectual property of Cambridge Assessment International Education.

Cross-curricular links	LB pages	WB pages	TG pages
English	103, Activity 3		123

Focus on how sounds are made

Learner's Book
pages 90–94

Workbook page 54

Unit 7 Slides 1–3
Unit 7 Flashcards
Visuals 33–34

Unit 7 Audio

Learning objectives

Revision of:

- **1Ps.01** *Identify different sources of sound.*
- **1Ps.02** *Explore that as sound travels from a source it becomes quieter.*
- **5Ps.01** Investigate how sounds are made by vibrating sources.
- **5TWSa.03** Make a conclusion from results informed by scientific understanding.
- **5TSWa.05** Present and interpret results using tables, bar charts, dot plots and line graphs.

Background information

The activities on pages 90 and 91 of the *Learner's Book* are designed to remind learners of prior learning relating to identifying sources of sound, and that as a sound travels from a source it becomes quieter.

The focus of pages 92 and 93 is to introduce the idea that sounds are made when objects vibrate. Even when you cannot see the vibrations and how loud and quiet sounds are made. If a sound is being produced, then something is vibrating. This is the basic concept behind this topic on sound, so make sure that learners know this idea before moving on, even if it means repeating activities or providing additional experiences of things vibrating. Most practical sound activities are better done outside where learners can make noise without disturbing other classes and where they can find space to hear the sounds that they are making.

Page 94 focuses on how sound travels from the source to the ear; when a drum is hit, the air particles next to the drum skin vibrate and collide with other particles. This vibration is then passed on from one particle to the next until it reaches the ear. Some learners hold the misconception that it is the particles that literally move from the sound source to the ear and 'carry' the sound.

Work safely ⚠

At the beginning of this topic explain to learners that they should never make a loud noise next to their own or anyone else's ear because it could damage their hearing.

Starter activity suggestions

- Take learners on a sound walk.
- Ask learners to put their fingers on their throat where the voice box is and gently hum and feel the voice box vibrate. Ask learners to make louder sounds and discuss how the vibration has changed. Focus on scaffolding the idea that when learners make a sound with their voices, their voice box vibrates. When they make a quiet sound, the vibration is small; when they make a louder sound the vibration gets bigger.
- Use Unit 7 Slide 2 (boost-learning.com) to discuss how vibrations create sounds.

⟳ Unit 7 Slide 2 answers

Making sounds

1 The girl's voice box is vibrating.

2 The drum skin is vibrating, making the rice jump.

3 The tuning fork is vibrating, making the water move.

4 The pneumatic drill is vibrating.

Activity notes and answers

Pages 90 and 91 Sources of sound
Activity 1
a–d Check that learners understand what sources of sound means.
Activity 2
a–c Take learners on a sound walk around the school both inside and outside. Challenge them to do so quietly and see who can identify the most sounds and the most unusual sounds.
Activity 3
This activity could be completed as a whole class on a walk outside the school grounds. Alternatively, it could be set as a home/school activity, with learners bringing their observations back to class to share.
Activity 4
a Yes. As they walked away from the sound, the sound got fainter until when at 50 m they could no longer hear the sound.
b They made the same sound each time, they measured every 10 m, recording what they could hear.
c–e Give learners time to carry out their fair test and record in the same way, so that they can compare their table with the one on page 91. Learners should find the same pattern in their results.

Page 92 How sounds are made
Activity 1
a–c When the tuning fork is tapped, learners will hear it make a sound. When the tuning fork is placed against the cheek and nose, its vibrations can be felt and learners will feel it 'tickle' their skin.
d and **e** When the tuning fork is tapped, a sound is heard. When it is placed in the container of water, the vibrations are transferred to the water, which causes it to 'splash'.
Activity 2
When the tuning fork is tapped, a sound is heard. When it is placed against the ping pong ball, the vibrations are transferred to the ball, which cause it to move.
Activity 3
a–c When the spatula or ruler is pulled down and let go, a sound can be heard when it vibrates.

Page 93 Volume – loud and quiet sounds
Activity 1
a–c Carry out this activity on the grass, using seed that birds will eat. Learners should observe that when the skin of the drum is hit, the skin vibrates; the drum makes a sound and the seed vibrates – bouncing on the drum.
Activity 2
Learners should notice that the harder the drum is hit, the bigger the vibration and the louder the sound. The more gently the drum is hit, the smaller the vibration and the quieter the sound. Help learners make the link between the size of the vibration and the volume of the sound. Check that learners use the word 'volume'.
Activity 3
The aim of this activity is for learners to feel the air above the drum vibrate. The harder the drum is hit, the louder the sound, the bigger the vibration is of the drum skin, and the more the air vibrates. The opposite is true when the drum is hit more gently. The vibration from the skin of the drum is transferred to the air, and the particles of air transfer the vibrations to the ears, which is how we hear.

Page 94 How sounds travel
Activity 1
The aim of this activity is to demonstrate to learners that sound travels. When they make a sound, they make the air in front of them vibrate. This vibration is passed on from air particle to air particle until it reaches the balloon. The balloon skin vibrates (and the air inside the balloon) so that the partner can feel the balloon vibrating. Check learners' diagrams and ask them to explain it to check their understanding.

Activity 2

a–f When the string is rubbed with the cloth, the string vibrates and produces a sound. This sound is quite faint. When the vibrations travel to the cup, the cup and the air vibrate. The sound is amplified and the air vibrations around the cup are transferred to our ears through the air and we can hear it. Learners should be able to explain most of this, although they might not realise that the cup amplifies (makes louder) the sound.

g Example: the sound will change.

h Example: type of cup, dry cloth, very wet cloth, type of cloth, change the string for wool.

i Ask learners whether their predictions were correct.

Further activities

- Ask learners to complete *Workbook* pages 55–56.
- Show learners Unit 7 Slide 3 (boost-learning.com) and discuss the line graph.

Unit 7 Slide 3 answers

Quick quiz

a Between 6 p.m. and 6 a.m. because the sound was the quietest, below 5 dB.

b Around 1 p.m. it could be lunch time, when learners would be noisier.

c Accept reasonable answers. Example: The school day is over and the school may be empty.

d Accept reasonable answers. Example: Learners could be leaving the school and going home or playing sport.

e Accept reasonable answers, getting learners to share and explain their sketches with a partner.

ICT links

Learners could explore measuring sound using sound meters or an app during the course of a lesson or a day.

Assessment ideas

Ask learners to write down three key things that they have learnt from the activities so far.

Workbook answers

Page 54 Sounds around us

1 Accept appropriate answers.

2 a The further away from the source of the sound, the quieter the sound.

b The closer you are to the source of the sound, the louder the sound.

Page 55 Testing how sounds are made

a The rice bounces on the cling film when the tin is hit.

b When the tin vibrates, it vibrates the air around it, which then vibrates the cling film, which makes the rice bounce.

c Hit the tin harder to make bigger vibrations.

d The harder the spoon hits the tin, the bigger the vibration and the higher the rice bounces. The softer the spoon hits the tin, the smaller the vibration so the rice does not bounce as high.

e No, stones are heavier than rice, so it would need a very big vibration to make the stones move.

Page 56 Measuring sound

1 a Space rocket launching at 180 dB.

b Ear mufflers/ear defenders to prevent their hearing from being damaged.

2 a Check that learners have correctly labelled the bars with the sources of sound.

   b Children were in the canteen having lunch, sound of plates, cutlery, children talking and moving about.

   c Car horn and noise in the canteen.

   d Examples: Yes, because the same things happen every day. No, because different things happen each day so the sound might be louder or quieter.

Success criteria

While completing the activities, assess and record learners.

Learning objectives	Success criteria
1Ps.01 *Identify different sources of sound.*	Learners can identify the sources of different sounds in their environment.
1Ps.02 *Explore that as sound travels from a source it becomes quieter.*	Learners can describe how a sound becomes fainter the further away you are from the source of the sound.
5Ps.01 Investigate how sounds are made by vibrating sources.	Learners can describe how sounds are made using the word *vibrations*.
5TWSa.03 Make a conclusion from results informed by scientific understanding.	Learners can use their understanding of sound to make conclusions.
5TSWa.05 Present and interpret results using bar charts, dot plots and line graphs.	Learners can present data in a bar chart.

Focus on drumming

Learner's Book
pages 95–97

Unit 7 Slides 4–5

Learning objectives

- **5Ps.01** Investigate how sounds are made by vibrating sources.
- **5Ps.02** Describe sounds in terms of high or low pitch and loud or quiet volume.

Background information

Page 95 of the *Learner's Book* is designed to consolidate learners' understanding of sound and vibrations through the application of what they know to design and make a drum using recyclable materials.

Unit 7 Slide 4 (boost-learning.com) introduces learners to the internationally famous musician Evelyn Glennie, who plays a variety of percussion instruments even though she is deaf. She hears the sound of, for example, the xylophone through her fingertips; that is, she feels the vibrations. She also removes her shoes and stands on a wooden platform when she plays, so that she can feel the vibrations produced by the music through her feet.

Page 96 introduces learners to how stringed instruments are played.

- Show learners Unit 7 Slide 4 (boost-learning.com) and discuss how Evelyn Glennie can 'hear' music even though she is deaf. If possible, give learners the opportunity at some point to wear headphones while they play a percussion instrument to find out if they can 'feel' the music through their fingertips.
- Play a video clip of Evelyn Glennie playing a xylophone or other percussion instrument.
- Take a selection of drums from the music room or department outdoors for learners to explore the sounds they make and how the volume of the sound can be changed.
- Invite a musician to give a performance playing the drums.

Unit 7 Slide 4 answers

Evelyn Glennie

Accept learners' responses.

Activity notes and answers

Page 95 Drumming
Activity 1

a–e Ask learners to discuss in their groups the different drums and how think they are made. Encourage them to apply this to their own drums. Make sure learners have access to a range of resources. Encourage them to play their drum as they make it, listening to the sound, and so on, so that they can make changes as they work. Remind learners to think about what will vibrate and how to change the volume of the sound. Engage learners in peer assessment where they watch each other demonstrate their drum, and listen to explanations of how the sounds are made and changed.

f Engage learners in listening to drumming on the internet. Take the class outdoors for a drumming session, using the drums they have made.

Page 96 Musical instruments around the world
Activity 1

a By plucking the strings (elastic bands).

b The strings (elastic bands) and the air around.

c Pluck harder to make a bigger vibration for a loud sound; pluck more softly to make a smaller vibration for a quiet sound.

d Lower

e Higher

f Check learners' pictures and captions.

Further activities

Learners could research further information about Evelyn Glennie. They could write a short 150-word biography for a school newsletter or website.

Assessment ideas

Show learners Unit 7 Slide 5 (boost-learning.com). Ask them to use their knowledge so far to answer the questions.

Unit 7 Slide 5 answers

Indian Sitar

a String

b The string is plucked. The string and the air around the sitar vibrate.

c Plucking the strings harder will change the volume, making the sound louder. Plucking the strings softly will change the volume making the sound quieter.

d Playing on thicker or thinner strings. Changing the tension (how tight or loose the string is).

Success criteria

While completing the activities, assess and record learners.

Learning objectives	Success criteria
5Ps.01 Investigate how sounds are made by vibrating sources.	Learners describe how a drum skin and guitar strings vibrate to make a sound.
5Ps.02 Describe sounds in terms of high or low pitch and loud or quiet volume.	Learners describe how hitting the drum skin or plucking guitar strings hard or gently changes the volume.

Focus on changing the pitch of a sound

Learner's Book
pages 97–100

Workbook pages 57–58

Unit 7 Slide 6
Visuals 35–36

Learning objectives

- **5Ps.01** Investigate how sounds are made by vibrating sources.
- **5Ps.02** Describe sounds in terms of high or low pitch and loud or quiet volume.
- **5Ps.03** Investigate how to change the volume and pitch of sounds.
- **5TWSc.06** Carry out practical work safely.
- **5TWSp.03** Make predictions, referring to relevant scientific knowledge and understanding within familiar and unfamiliar contexts.
- **5TWSa.02** Describe patterns in results, including identifying any anomalous results.

Background information

The purpose of activities on pages 97–100 of the *Learner's Book* is to extend learners' experience and knowledge of sound in the context of string instruments and bottle xylophones. On page 97, learners are introduced to the term 'pitch'. Pitch is how high or low a sound is. Some learners confuse volume and pitch, so singing high notes and low notes, quiet and loud, then quiet high notes and loud low notes with the class helps to clarify the terms. Learners explore pitch and how to change both the pitch and volume of sounds.

Pitch is how high or low a sound is. In a string instrument there are three main rules for learners to know:

- The tighter the string, the higher the sound; the slacker the string, the lower the sound.
- The longer the string, the lower the sound; the shorter the string, the higher the sound.
- The thicker the string, the lower the sound; the thinner the string, the higher the sound.

In the water xylophone, the length of the column of water determines the pitch. When the glass is hit, the longer the column of water the lower the pitch; the shorter the column the higher the pitch.

It is different though if one blows across the bottles, since it is the air in the bottles that is vibrating. The amount of water in the bottle shortens or lengthens the column of air in the bottle. The shorter the column of air, the higher the pitch of the sound; the longer the column of air, the lower the sound.

Starter activity suggestions

- Give learners access to string instruments and water xylophones so that they can explore playing them and changing both volume and pitch. Remind them that pitch is how high or low a sound is. Ask them to work out what the rules are for changing pitch. Use the activities in this section to either substantiate or challenge their ideas.

- Invite musicians (these could be members of staff or learners) to demonstrate playing different string and wind instruments and explain changing pitch.

- Use Unit 7 Slide 6 (boost-learning.com).

Unit 7 Slide 6 answers

Bottle xylophone

a The glass and the water.
b By hitting the bottle harder.
c Hit bottles that have different amounts of water in them: higher pitch = less water, lower pitch = more water.
d The air in the bottles vibrates.

Activity notes and answers

Page 97 Changing the pitch of a sound
Activity 1

Observe learners demonstrating to their partner and listen to their explanations, challenging learners to use the appropriate scientific vocabulary.

Activity 2

Learners design and make their guitar. Learners should practise for their video, including writing a script explaining how they made their guitar and how it works, using scientific concepts and words that they have learnt so far in this unit. Engage learners in peer assessment where they comment on each other's descriptions and explanations.

Page 98 More about changing the pitch of a sound
Activity 1

Learners should have time to explore changing the sound so that they can then predict what will happen with confidence. Check that their diagrams show the ruler vibrating and their explanation of how to change the pitch. Help them to apply this to string instruments.

Activity 2

a–c Check learners set up the bottle xylophone correctly.
d The pitch gets higher and lower.
e The more water in the bottle, the lower the pitch. The less water in the bottle, the higher the pitch of the sound.
f The sound is different.
g The pitch of the sound is different.

Work safely

Remind learners to take care when hitting the glass with a spoon.

Page 99 Volume and pitch in wind instruments
Activity 1
Learners should be able to describe that the air in the bottle is vibrating, as well as that the longer the column of air, the lower the pitch and the shorter the column of air, the higher the pitch. Learners should be able to explain that changing the column of air changes the pitch of the sound.

Page 100 Making pan pipes
Activity 1

a–d Check that learners measure the straws and make their pan pipes correctly.

e–h Give learners time to play their pan pipes and explore changing both pitch and volume of the sound. They should be able to explain that the harder they blow the louder the sound because the air is vibrating more and that when blowing gently the air vibrates less and the sound is quieter. They should also be able to explain that it is the length of the column of air in each of the pipes that changes the pitch. The shorter the column of air, the higher the pitch and the longer the column, the lower the pitch.

i Listen to learners' explanations of how this changed the sounds, checking that they are using scientific words correctly.

Further activities

● Give learners time to either compose and play a tune that they already know and share with the rest of the class.

● Ask learners to complete *Workbook* pages 57 and 58.

ICT links

Learners can use decibel meters or an app to measure the volume of their instruments.

Assessment ideas

Listen to learners' explanations as an opportunity for formative assessment to check their understanding.

Workbook answers

Page 57 Changing the pitch of the sound of a cereal packet guitar

1 a The pitch of the sound got higher.
   b At 1
   c At 5
   d The thicker the elastic band, the lower the pitch of the sound. The thinner the elastic band, the higher the pitch of the sound.
   e The tighter the elastic band, the higher the pitch of the sound.
   f Pluck the strings harder; this would make bigger vibrations and a louder sound.
   g Pluck the strings more gently; this would make smaller vibrations and a quieter sound.

Page 58 Water xylophone

1 a The water
   b The bottle with the least water had the highest pitch. The bottle with the most water had the lowest pitch.

2 a The column of air in the bottle.
   b The bottle with the shortest column of air had the highest pitch. The bottle with the longest column of air had the lowest pitch.
   c Check learners' responses.

3 Add more water so that the column of air becomes shorter and the pitch will become higher.

4 The column of air in the pipes vibrates. The pitch is changed by changing the length of the pipe (and so the column of air). The volume is changed by blowing more softly (quieter) or harder (louder).

While completing the activities, assess and record learners.

Learning objectives	Success criteria
5Ps.01 Investigate how sounds are made by vibrating sources.	Learners can explain how sounds are made in different instruments.
5Ps.02 Describe sounds in terms of high or low pitch and loud or quiet volume.	Learners can describe pitch and volume in different instruments.
5Ps.03 Investigate how to change the volume and pitch of sounds.	Learners can change the volume and pitch of sounds in different instruments.
5TWSc.06 Carry out practical work safely.	Learners can safely hit a spoon against glass.
5TWSp.03 Make predictions, referring to relevant scientific knowledge and understanding within familiar and unfamiliar contexts.	Learners can make predictions about how sounds travel and the pitch of sound different lengths of a ruler makes.
5TWSa.02 Describe patterns in results, including identifying any anomalous results.	Learners can describe the pattern between the amount of water in a bottle and the pitch of sound it makes when hit.

Focus on world instruments

Learner's Book
pages 101–103

Workbook pages 59–62

Worksheet 13
Worksheet 14

Unit 7 Flashcards
Visual 37

Unit 7 Audio

Learning objectives

- **5Ps.01** Investigate how sounds are made by vibrating sources.
- **5Ps.02** Describe sounds in terms of high or low pitch and loud or quiet volume.
- **5Ps.03** Investigate how to change the volume and pitch of sounds.
- **5TWSc.07** Use a range of secondary information sources to research and select relevant evidence to answer questions.

Background information

The purpose of pages 101–103 of the *Learner's Book* is to give learners the opportunity to learn about different instruments from around the world and apply what they have learnt about sound in this unit. There are over 1 500 different kinds of musical instruments from across the world that fall into basic categories of woodwind, percussion, strings, brass and keyboard. Science teaches us how sounds are made and how they can be changed. Musicians use this knowledge to put those sounds together to create melodies and songs. These cross-curricular links are important, so do help learners to make connections between the two subjects. If possible, work with the music department so that learners have access to a range of instruments and have support when making their own.

Starter activity suggestions

- Show learners a series of video clips of instruments from across the world being played. Ask learners to vote for their favourite.
- Borrow different instruments for learners to explore and work out how the sounds are made, how to change pitch and volume.

Activity notes and answers

Page 101 Science in context: Music around the world
Activity 1

a Give learners time to carry out this research, groups could delegate instruments to different members and then share their research.

b Learners could create three slides showing each of the instruments they have researched and the information.

Page 102 Musical band
Activity 1

This activity will require time for learners to work as a group to design and make their instruments. Make sure that learners apply their knowledge of how sounds are made and changed to their instruments. It is a good idea to get learners to share their planning with the class or another group before they make their instruments and receive feedback that could support them in how they make them. This could also become a home/school activity with family members supporting learners in making their instruments. Once completed the class could perform for other learners in the school to celebrate their work.

Page 103 What have you learnt about sound?
Activity 1

a The strings, air around and the wood of the oud.

b To change the volume, pluck the strings harder to make bigger vibrations and a louder sound and pluck softer to make smaller vibrations for a quieter sound.

c To change the pitch, make the length of the string longer (low pitch) and shorter (high pitch).

d The sound would become fainter.

Activity 2

a The air in the bottles would vibrate and make a sound.

b The bottle with the shortest column of air.

c The bottle with the longest column of air.

Activity 3

This activity creates cross-curricular links to English and ESL.

Vibration: When something moves back and forwards from side to side or up and down quickly.

Volume: How loud or quiet a sound is.

Pitch: How high or low a sound is.

Column of air: The length of the air in a cylinder, for example in pan pipes.

Wind instrument: A musical instrument where the sound is made by blowing into the instrument and vibrating the air inside.

Further activities

- Ask learners to complete *Workbook* pages 59–61.
- Give learners Worksheets 13 and 14 (boost-learning.com) that challenges them to apply their understanding of sound.

Worksheet 13 answers

World instrument	Name	Country	Changing volume and pitch
	guiro	Any South American country, including Cuba	Scrape harder to increase volume. Pitch of this instrument cannot be changed.
	Didgeridoo	Australia	Blowing harder will increase volume. The shorter the didgeridoo the higher the pitch.
	Finger cymbals	Middle Eastern or Asian countries, including Pakistan	Tapping them harder will increase volume. The thicker or wider the cymbal changes the lower the pitch.
	Lyra	Crete (Greece)	Pluck strings harder to increase the volume or increase the pressure of the bow. Move the finger up and down the string to shorten or lengthen pitch. The longer the string, the lower the note.
	Tar drum	Saudi Arabia	Hit the drum harder to increase the volume. To change the pitch, tighten the skin, hit closer to the centre of the drum, put a thicker skin on the drum.

Worksheet 14 answers

1 Example: A mouse makes a higher pitch sound because it is smaller.
2 a Percussion
  b The metal cones, the air around them.
  c The biggest cone will make the high pitch sound; it has a longer column of air.
  The smallest cone will make the low pitch sound; it has a shorter column of air.

3 Example: Sound travels through air because the particles vibrate against each other and the vibrations are passed to the ear. In space there is no air, so vibrations cannot travel to the ear.
4 a True. If learners answer false encourage them to research this. In fact a baby's cry can reach 115 dB, which is louder than a car's horn.
  b True. The loudest sound is a volcanic eruption.
5 An echo is a sound that is repeated because the sound bounces back off a smooth, hard surface. Accept either an image copied from a book or the internet or their own drawing that shows the sound bouncing back.

Workbook answers

Page 59 Changing sounds

1 a Sounds can be loud or soft. This is called <u>volume</u>.
  b Elastic bands can make sounds. You can change the <u>volume</u> of the sound by changing how hard you pull the elastic bands.
  c When you change the thickness of the elastic bands, you change how high or <u>low</u> the sound is.
  d Changing sounds to make them lower or higher is called changing the <u>pitch</u> of a sound.
  e The <u>volume</u> of a sound is how loud or how soft the sound is.

2 a Pluck the strings harder.
  b Pluck the strings more gently.
  c Change the thickness of the elastic bands, for example, thinner or thicker or a mixture.
  d Change the length of the elastic bands or how taut (tight) they are.

Page 60 What vibrates?

1 a In a drum, the <u>skin</u> vibrates to make a sound.
  b In a guitar, the <u>string</u> vibrates to make a sound.
  c In pan pipes, the <u>air</u> vibrates to make a sound.

2 a Check that the shortest straw is labelled.
  b Check that the longest straw is labelled.
  c Blow harder over the pipes so that the air vibrates more.
  d Blow softly over the pipes so that the air vibrates gently.
  e Blow hard over a short pipe with a short column of air.
  f Blow gently over a long pipe with a long column of air.

Page 61 Spoon gong

1 a The sound of the spoon vibrating against the table, but it might sound different.
  b The spoon hits the table, the spoon vibrates, and the vibration travels along the string and into the ears where the sound is heard.
  c Hit the spoon harder on the table to make a bigger vibration that will increase the volume of the sound.

ICT links

- Learners video their performances.
- Learners use the internet to research different instruments.
- Learners create PowerPoint slides of their musical instruments.

Assessment ideas

- Use the Flashcards and Audio recordings (boost-learning.com) to assess that learners know and understand the new words and concepts covered in this unit.
- Ask learners to complete the checklist on page 101 of the *Learner's Book*, and the self-check activity on page 62 of the *Workbook*.

Success criteria

While completing the activities, assess and record learners.

Learning objectives	Success criteria
5Ps.01 Investigate how sounds are made by vibrating sources.	Learners can explain how sounds are made in different instruments.
5Ps.02 Describe sounds in terms of high or low pitch and loud or quiet volume.	Learners can describe pitch and volume in different instruments.
5Ps.03 Investigate how to change the volume and pitch of sounds.	Learners can change the volume and pitch of sounds in different instruments.
5TWSc.07 Use a range of secondary information sources to research and select relevant evidence to answer questions.	Learners research information about different world instruments.

Unit 8 Magnetism

Learning objectives from Stages 1–4	LB pages	WB pages	TG pages
3Pe.01 Describe magnets as having a north pole and a south pole.	104–105, 106–108		128–30, 130–133
3Pe.02 Describe how magnets interact when near each other, using the terms repel and attract.	104–105, 106–108		128–130, 130–133
3Pe.03 Investigate how some materials are magnetic but many are not.	104–105	63	128–130

Learning objectives overview

Physics	Online resources	LB pages	WB pages	TG pages
Electricity and magnetism	Flashcards/Audio			
5Pe.01 Know the difference between a magnet and a magnetic material.		106–108	63	130–133
5Pe.02 Know that forces act over a distance between magnets, and between a magnet and a magnetic material.	Unit 8 Slide 4	106–108		130–133
5Pe.03 Know that magnets can have different magnetic strengths.		109–110	66	133–135

Thinking and Working Scientifically	LB pages	WB pages	TG pages
Purpose and planning			
5TWSp.03 Make predictions, referring to relevant scientific knowledge and understanding within familiar and unfamiliar contexts.	108, Activity 1 111, Activity 1	65	130–133, 133–135
5TWSp.04 Plan fair test investigations, identifying the independent, dependent and control variables.	105, Activity 1 108, Activity 1 110, Activity 1 111, Activity 1	65	128–130, 130–133, 133–135
Carrying out scientific enquiry			
5TWSc.01 Sort, group and classify objects, materials and living things through testing, observation and using secondary information.	105, Activity 1		128–130
5TWSc.04 Decide when observations and measurements need to be repeated to give more reliable data.	111, Activity 1		133–135
5TWSc.05 Take appropriately accurate measurements.	110, Activity 2		133–135
5TWSc.08 Collect and record observations and/or measurements in tables and diagrams appropriate to the type of scientific enquiry.	111, Activity 1		133–135
Analysis, evaluation and conclusions			
5TWSa.01 Describe the accuracy of predictions, based on results.	111, Activity 2		133–135
5TWSa.03 Make a conclusion from results informed by scientific understanding.	105, Activity 1–3 110, Activity 2 111, Activity 2		128–130, 133–135
5TWSa.04 Suggest how an investigation could be improved and explain any proposed changes.	110, Let's talk		133–135
5TWSa.05 Present and interpret results using tables, bar charts, dot plots and line graphs.	108, Activity 1 110, Activity 2	66	130–133, 133–135

Science in Context	LB pages	WB pages	TG pages
5SIC.02 Describe how science is used in their local area.	112		136
5SIC.04 Identify people who use science, including professionally, in their area and describe how they use science.	112		136

These learning objectives are reproduced from the Cambridge Primary Science curriculum framework (0097) from 2020. This Cambridge International copyright material is reproduced under licence and remains the intellectual property of Cambridge Assessment International Education.

Cross-curricular links	LB pages	WB pages	TG pages
Mathematics	106, Activity 2 110, Activity 1–2		131 134

Focus on exploring magnets

Learner's Book
pages 104–105

Workbook page 63

Unit 8 Slides 1–2
Unit 8 Flashcards

Unit 8 Audio

Learning objectives

Revision of:
- **3Pe.01** Describe magnets as having a north pole and a south pole.
- **3Pe.02** Describe how magnets interact when near each other, using the terms repel and attract.
- **3Pe.03** Investigate how some materials are magnetic but many are not.
- **5TWSc.01** Sort, group and classify objects, materials and living things through testing, observation and using secondary information.
- **5TWSa.03** Make a conclusion from results informed by scientific understanding.
- **5TWSp.04** Plan fair test investigations, identifying the independent, dependent and control variables.

Background information

The purpose of the activities on pages 104 and 105 of the *Learner's Book* is for learners to recap on their prior knowledge and experiences of magnets from earlier stages. Learners create a mind map to organise what they know about magnets. Each 'arm' of the map is a different section about magnets. Learners can create as many 'arms' as they want; for example, one for 'Materials', 'Types of magnets', and so on.

To help 'cue' learners into prior learning let them explore magnets and a range of materials to help remind them of past learning. You might also want to include key vocabulary such as 'magnets', 'repel', 'attract'. As learners work through this unit, they should return at regular intervals to add new learning to their mind map.

Starter activity suggestions

- Give learners a range of magnets and materials to explore to remind them of what they already know and some things that they did not.
- Show learners Unit 8 Slide 2 (boost-learning.com) and use it to explain how to make a mind map.

Unit 8 Slide 2 answers

Magnets

Use the slide to explain mind mapping. Check that learners understand how to set out their mind map.

Activity notes and answers

Page 104 Exploring magnets
Activity 1
At this stage correcting errors may not be necessary since as learners work through this unit, they should be able to look back and revise errors. Give learners time to visit other groups and take ideas from them to add to their own mind map.

Page 105 The language of magnets
Activity 1
This test will require samples of different metals. These could include screws, coins, aluminium foil, copper wire. A basic test would be for learners to test and sort the metals into magnetic and non-magnetic. They should conclude that Jin's prediction is incorrect, magnets only attract certain metals. While learners usually only come across iron and steel, there are, in fact, four metals (and their alloys) that are magnetic, i.e. iron, steel, nickel and cobalt.

Activity 2
a Magnets push each other away or pull towards each other.
b Attract and repel.
c and **d** Learners should peer assess each other's diagrams and annotations.

Activity 3
a When north and south poles are put near each other, they attract. When the same poles are put near each other, they repel.
b Scaffold thinking if some learners are unable to correctly check their partner's work. Suggest that they use magnets to see if their partner is correct.

Further activities

- Learners add additional information to their mind maps.
- Ask learners to complete *Workbook* page 63.

Assessment ideas

The mind map provides a useful formative assessment point to find out what learners remember and understand and whether some of the concepts from the earlier stages require additional revision.

Workbook answers

Page 63 Do magnets attract all metals?
1 Magnetic: tin can, steel hammer, iron and steel screw
  Non-magnetic: aluminium drinks can, gold necklace, copper wire
2 Check that learners use a magnetic object for the maze.
3 A magnet can repel and attract another magnet. A magnetic object can only attract a magnet.

Success criteria

While completing the activities, assess and record learners.

Learning objectives	Success criteria
3Pe.01 Describe magnets as having a north pole and a south pole.	Learners can say that a magnet has a north and south pole.
3Pe.02 Describe how magnets interact when near each other, using the terms repel and attract.	Learners can describe how magnets attract and repel each other.

Learning objectives	Success criteria
3Pe.03 *Investigate how some materials are magnetic but many are not.*	Learners can test materials to find out if they are magnetic or not.
5TWSc.01 Sort, group and classify objects, materials and living things through testing, observation and using secondary information.	Learners can sort materials into magnetic and non-magnetic.
5TWSa.03 Make a conclusion from results informed by scientific understanding.	Learners can make conclusions by exploring with magnets.
5TWSp.04 Plan fair test investigations, identifying the independent, dependent and control variables.	Learners can design a fair test investigation to prove if magnets attract all metals.

Focus on north and south poles

Learner's Book
pages 106–108

Workbook pages 64–65

Unit 8 Slides 3–5
Visual 38

Learning objectives

Revision of:
- *3Pe.01 Describe magnets as having a north pole and a south pole.*
- *3Pe.02 Describe how magnets interact when near each other, using the terms repel and attract.*
- **5Pe.01** Know the difference between a magnet and a magnetic material.
- **5Pe.02** Know that forces act over a distance between magnets, and between a magnet and a magnetic material.
- **5TWSp.03** Make predictions, referring to relevant scientific knowledge and understanding within familiar and unfamiliar contexts.
- **5TWSp.04** Plan fair test investigations, identifying the independent, dependent and control variables.
- **5TWSa.03** Make a conclusion from results informed by scientific understanding.
- **5TWSa.05** Present and interpret results using tables, bar charts, dot plots and line graphs.

Background information

The purpose of the activities on page 106 of the *Learner's Book* is to further develop learners' understanding of the concept of north and south poles on a magnet. Learners will use this knowledge to explore the poles on magnets and predict what will happen when poles are put together.

Each magnet has a north and south pole. On a bar magnet they are at either end of the magnet, on a ring magnet on either side, and on a horseshoe magnet at the end of each part of the 'shoe'. A simple rule is that like poles repel and unlike poles attract. Some magnets have the letter N and S on them, others have a dot.

The activities on page 107 introduce learners to the idea of a magnetic field. A magnetic field is the area around a magnet where the force of the magnet acts on another magnet of magnetic materials. One way to show the effect of a magnetic field is to use iron filings. However, it is important that these are used in a transparent sealed container since the filings are small enough to be inhaled. Activities on page 108 provide an opportunity for learners to explore the idea that a magnetic force can work through materials.

Starter activity suggestions

- Show learners Unit 8 Slides 3–5 (boost-learning.com) to help explain key ideas relating to north and south poles on magnets and the magnetic field.
- Give learners time to explore putting poles of a magnet near each other.
- Give learners iron filings in transparent sealed containers to explore observing the effect of the magnetic fields of different magnets.

Unit 8 Slide 3 answers

a The poles on the horseshoe magnet are on either ends of the horseshoe, on the ring magnet they are on the top and bottom and on the bar magnet on the two ends.
b Like poles repel and unlike poles attract.
c When learners have completed their diagrams, they should peer assess each other's responses.

Unit 8 Slide 4 answers

a The magnetic field around a magnet.
b Because the field has different strengths around the magnet.
c The ends of the magnet because the lines are closer together.
d Because a magnet does not have to touch an object made from magnetic material to make it move. It does not need to have contact with the object.

Unit 8 Slide 5 answers

The Earth is a magnet

a Both have a magnetic field around them, shown by the lines. Some lines are closer together and others further apart.
b and c Strongest is where the lines are closer together (at the North and South Poles), weakest where the lines are further apart (around the equator).

Activity notes and answers

Page 106 North and south poles
Activity 1
Ask learners to think of a way to remember that like poles repel and unlike attract – they could create a saying or a hand signal.
Activity 2
This activity creates cross-curricular links with measurement in Mathematics. Discuss with learners how they know that the magnet has a magnetic field that they cannot see. Explain that scientists call the force of a magnet a non-contact force, because the magnet does not have to touch the paper clip to make it move (unlike a push or a pull which are contact forces).

Page 107 How do we know there is a magnetic field?
Activity 1
Check learners' understanding and their diagrams.

Page 108 Marvellous magnets
Activity 1
a–c Learners could change the material, keep the distance and paper clip the same, and record results in the table including their predictions and results.

d and **e** Challenge learners to reflect on why some predictions were incorrect. For example, had they underestimated the strength of the magnetic field?

f Check that learners' conclusions match their results.

Challenge yourself!

Learners could plan to use a bowl of water or a plastic bottle filled with water and a magnetic object inside. They could also try this out at home.

Further activities

Ask learners to complete *Workbook* pages 64 and 65.

ICT links

Learners could record magnetic field patterns by photographing them for their books.

Assessment ideas

Get learners to return to their mind maps and add new information from their learning so far, challenge them to use appropriate scientific vocabulary.

Workbook answers

Page 64 Magnetic field

1 a The force field is strongest at each end of the bar magnet.

b There are lots of iron filings at each end.

c The force field is weakest at the middle of the bar magnet.

d There are not as many iron filings.

2 a Magnet A

b It has the most iron filings.

Page 65 What does a magnet's magnetic field work through?

1 Check learners' predictions and their test design.

2 Check learners' predictions and their test design, challenging them to include measurements.

Success criteria

While completing the activities, assess and record learners.

Learning objectives	Success criteria
3Pe.01 *Describe magnets as having a north pole and a south pole.*	Learners can say that a magnet has a north and south pole.
3Pe.02 *Describe how magnets interact when near each other, using the terms repel and attract.*	Learners can describe how magnets attract and repel each other.
5Pe.01 Know the difference between a magnet and a magnetic material.	Learners can describe the difference between a magnet and a magnetic object.
5Pe.02 Know that forces act over a distance between magnets, and between a magnet and a magnetic material.	Learners can describe how forces act over a distance.
5TWSp.03 Make predictions, referring to relevant scientific knowledge and understanding within familiar and unfamiliar contexts.	Learners can make predictions about which materials will allow the magnetic field to work through it.

Learning objectives	Success criteria
5TWSp.04 Plan fair test investigations, identifying the independent, dependent and control variables.	Learners can plan a fair test using magnets.
5TWSa.03 Make a conclusion from results informed by scientific understanding.	Learners can use their results and knowledge about magnets to make a conclusion.
5TWSa.05 Present and interpret results using tables, bar charts, dot plots and line graphs.	Learners can present their results in a table.

Focus on working like a scientist

Learner's Book
pages 109–111

Workbook page 66

Learning objectives

- **5Pe.03** Know that magnets can have different magnetic strengths.
- **5TWSp.03** Make predictions, referring to relevant scientific knowledge and understanding within familiar and unfamiliar contexts.
- **5TWSp.04** Plan fair test investigations, identifying the independent, dependent and control variables.
- **5TWSc.04** Decide when observations and measurements need to be repeated to give more reliable data.
- **5TWSc.05** Take appropriately accurate measurements.
- **5TWSa.03** Make a conclusion from results informed by scientific understanding.
- **5TWSc.08** Collect and record observations and/or measurements in tables and diagrams appropriate to the type of scientific enquiry.
- **5TWSa.01** Describe the accuracy of predictions, based on results.
- **5TWSa.04** Suggest how an investigation could be improved and explain any proposed changes.
- **5TWSa.05** Present and interpret results using tables, bar charts, dot plots and line graphs.

Background information

The focus of pages 109–111 of the *Learner's Book* is to develop learners' understanding of the need for measurement in science. It is easy for learners to fall into the trap of only using paper clips as a measurement tool when working with magnets. The problem with this approach is that at this level learners should be working like scientists and using standard measures. Standard units do not vary from country to country and therefore can be used to make comparisons. As everyone is using the same language, it ensures uniformity and scientists can share data, understand the numbers involved and also repeat and compare tests. This set of activities aims to help learners understand why using standard measurements is important in science and therefore help them to value the power of the numbers and data that they collect. This also helps to make their data more useable and reliable to other scientists.

Starter activity suggestions

Use the pages at the beginning of the *Learner's Book* on *Thinking and working like a scientist* and discuss what learners think makes a good scientist. Focus on the idea of using measurement and its importance.

Activity notes and answers

Page 109 Science in context: Working like scientists
Let's talk

Listen to learners' responses. Do learners appreciate that even though they carried out a fair test and recorded results clearly using a table because they used paper clips, and paper clips of different sizes they would not be able to compare data and draw valid conclusions? They were not working like real scientists who would have used standard measurements.

Page 110 Do magnets have different strengths?
Let's talk

The main change would be to use standard measures; for example use a scale to calculate the mass of the paper clips in grams, measure how far away in centimetres from the paper clip the magnet was before the paper clip moved.

Activity 1

This activity creates cross-curricular links with standard measurements in Mathematics.
Check learners' plans focusing on how they will measure and which standard measures they will use.
Some learners might suggest repeating readings to make sure that their results are believable (valid). Give learners time to look at each other's plans and peer assess giving each other feedback on their plans.

Activity 2

This activity creates cross-curricular links with bar charts in Mathematics. Check learners' work focusing on the measurements collected and their ability to use their data to draw a bar chart. Ask the class to compare activities where non-standard and standard measures were carried out. Ask: *What are the advantages of using the latter? How does it improve your work and make you a better scientist?* Learners carry out the fair test investigation that they planned in Activity 1.

Page 111 Do magnetic forces work over a distance?
Activity 1

Check the way learners are planning to work, challenging them to explain their approach and prediction (is it based on experience?). The measurements will be length and learners need to decide if they need to work in cm or mm and if repeating readings will be useful. Repeating readings would also help to verify (confirm) their results, to check that they are all around the same number and there are no anomalous (unusual) readings.

Activity 2

Challenge learners to think about how they will organise their report to make it interesting for someone else to read, for example using photographs, bullet points, sentences, tables, graphs, and so on. As with other activities, engage learners in peer assessment of each other's reports leaving comments on what they think is good and something that they could change/improve.

Further activities

- Give learners some unusual magnets to explore like marble magnets and magnetic strips, challenging them to find out how they work.
- Ask learners to complete *Workbook* page 66.

✏️ Workbook answers

Page 66 Which is the strongest magnet?

1 Check learners' bar charts. (Learners should draw a draft of their bar chart in the *Workbook* and redraw a neat version on a sheet of graph paper.)

2 a No, because the bar magnet picked up paper clips with a mass of 32 g but the cylinder picked up more (42 g).

b They weighed the paper clips to make sure that they were using standard measurements so their test could be repeated and so that other scientists understood the measurements.

c Type of paper clip, height the magnet was held over the paper clips.

d Type of magnet.

ICT links

Learners communicate their work as a PowerPoint presentation, a report or newspaper article.

Assessment ideas

- Learners add to the magnet mind map.
- Learners carry out peer assessments on each other's work.

Success criteria

While completing the activities, assess and record learners.

Learning objectives	Success criteria
5Pe.03 Know that magnets can have different magnetic strengths.	Learners can explain that magnets have different strengths.
5TWSp.03 Make predictions, referring to relevant scientific knowledge and understanding within familiar and unfamiliar contexts.	Learners can make predictions about how far the magnet can be away from an object and still attract it.
5TWSp.04 Plan fair test investigations, identifying the independent, dependent and control variables.	Learners can plan a fair test using magnets.
5TWSc.04 Decide when observations and measurements need to be repeated to give more reliable data.	Learners can decide when to repeat readings and explain why.
5TWSc.05 Take appropriately accurate measurements.	Learners measure accurately using appropriate standard measurements.
5TWSc.08 Collect and record observations and/or measurements in tables and diagrams appropriate to the type of scientific enquiry.	Learners can record data in a table.
5TWSa.01 Describe the accuracy of predictions, based on results.	Learners can say how accurate their predictions are.
5TWSa.04 Suggest how an investigation could be improved and explain any proposed changes.	Learners can describe how to improve an investigation.
5TWSa.03 Make a conclusion from results informed by scientific understanding.	Learners can use their results and knowledge about magnets to make a conclusion.
5TWSa.05 Present and interpret results using tables, bar charts, dot plots and line graphs.	Learners can present their results in a bar chart.

Focus on fascinating facts about magnetism

Learner's Book
pages 112–113

Workbook pages 67–68

Worksheet 15
Worksheet 16

Unit 8 Slide 6
Unit 8 Flashcards
Visual 39

Unit 8 Audio

Learning objectives

- **5SIC.02** Describe how science is used in their local area.
- **5SIC.04** Identify people who use science, including professionally, in their area and describe how they use science.

Background information

Page 112 of the *Learner's Book* is a *Science in context* activity that focuses on how the understanding of magnets is used both locally and internationally by people who are engaged in scientific activity. Over the years, scientists have been curious about how things work and have made connections between what they have found out about different phenomena and magnetism. Learners are introduced to the power of magnetars, the idea that the Earth has its own magnetic field and that animals can sense the Earth's magnetic field and use it to help them navigate. Unit 8 Slide 6 (boost-learning.com) shows how electromagnets are used to sort and recycle metals and other materials. Placing learning into context helps learners to develop an understanding that their science is used by different people for a range of reasons.

Starter activity suggestions

- Discuss the idea that scientists all over the world use the science that learners are learning to make sense of things that happen in space, in the animal world and to create, for example, machinery that carries out useful jobs.
- Show learners Unit 8 Slide 6 (boost-learning.com).

Unit 8 Slide 6 answers

The machine is an electro-magnet that can be switched on and off. It is used to sort metal (iron and steel) in scrapyards so that different materials can be recycled.

Activity notes and answers

Page 112 Science in context: Magnetism in space
Let's talk
Engage learners in discussion based on PMIs, *Positives* (what is good/helpful about it), *Minuses* (what is not so good) and *Interesting* (fascinating or out of the ordinary). Give learners time to discuss and collect their ideas, these could be scribed by groups onto large sheets of paper and displayed around the classroom so that groups can visit and add their ideas.

Page 113 What have you learnt about magnets?
Activity 1
a False   b True   c False   d False   e False   f False

Activity 2
Check learners' diagrams against the example of a force field diagram on page 107 of the *Learner's Book*.

Activity 3

A repel

B attract

C repel

Further activities

- Challenge learners to find unusual uses of magnets or fascinating facts and share with the rest of the class.
- Ask learners to complete *Workbook* pages 67–68. This can be used as formative assessment.
- Give learners Worksheets 15 and 16 (boost-learning.com) that challenge them to further apply their understanding and also carry out additional research on magnetism.

Workbook answers

Page 67 North and south poles

1 Check the saying that learners have created.

2 To make the magnet move he would have to use another magnet and make sure that the same poles are brought together. This is because the same poles repel, so the magnet would move about on top of the ball.

Page 68 Magnetism crossword

1	2	3	4	5	6	7	8	9	10	11	12
									[4]F		
[1]M	A	G	N	E	T				O		
A								[2]I	R	O	N
G			[5]A				[6]S		C		
[3]N	O	R	T	H	(grey)	P	O	L	E		
E			T				U				
T			R				T		F		
A			A				H		I		
E			C						E		
R			T						L		
									D		

Worksheet 15 answers

1 a Magnetic sweepers act like a brush but have a magnet instead of bristles and picks up objects on the floor made from iron and steel.

  b Airports use these to make sure that there are no dangerous iron and steel objects on the landing strip that could damage a plane.

  c To pick up iron and steel metal bits off the floor.

2 a They would separate magnetic materials from rocks.

  b To pick the stainless steel knives, forks and spoons off the dirty plates.

3 A simple compass can be made by magnetising a needle by stroking it with a magnet.

Worksheet 16 answers

1 Remind learners how to create an acrostic. Get learners to share and comment on each other's acrostic.

2 Michael Farraday discovered electromagnetism.

3 Display learners' artwork.

ICT links

Learners research magnets using the internet.

Assessment ideas

- Ask learners to complete their mind maps adding anything else they have learnt/found out about magnets.
- Use the Flashcards and Audio recordings (boost-learning.com) to assess that learners know and understand the new words and concepts covered in this unit.
- Ask learners to complete the checklist on page 113 of the *Learner's Book*, and the self-check activity on page 69 of the *Workbook*.

Success criteria

While completing the activities, assess and record learners.

Learning objectives	Success criteria
5SIC.02 Describe how science is used in their local area.	Learners can talk about what they know about magnets in their own lives and local area.
5SIC.04 Identify people who use science, including professionally, in their area and describe how they use science.	Learners can talk about how scientists have used science to work out how some things work.

Unit 9　Planet Earth

Learning objectives overview

Earth and Space	Online resources	LB pages	WB pages	TG pages
Planet Earth	Flashcards/Audio			
5ESp.01 Know that the Earth is surrounded by a layer of air called the atmosphere, which is a mixture of different gases (including nitrogen, carbon dioxide and oxygen).	Worksheet 17	115	70	140–141
5ESp.02 Understand that most water on Earth is not pure and has dissolved substances in it.		120–122		145–148
5ESp.03 Understand that pollution is the introduction of substances by humans that harm the environment and identify examples of pollution.	Unit 9 Slides 4–8	120–122, 123–125		145–148, 148–150
Cycles on Earth				
5ESc.01 Describe the water cycle (limited to evaporation, condensation and precipitation).	Unit 9 Slide 3 Worksheet 18	116–119	71–73	142–145

Thinking and Working Scientifically	LB pages	WB pages	TG pages
Models and representations			
5TWSm.01 Know that a model presents an object, process or idea in a way that shows some of the important features.	118, Activity 1	73	142–145
5TWSm.02 Use models, including diagrams, to represent and describe scientific phenomena and ideas.	118, Activity 1	73	142–145
Purpose and planning			
5TWSp.02 Know the features of the five main types of scientific enquiry.	122, Let's talk		145–148
Carrying out scientific enquiry			
5TWSc.03 Choose equipment to carry out an investigation and use it appropriately.	122, Let's talk		145–148
5TWSc.04 Decide when observations and measurements need to be repeated to give more reliable data.	122, Let's talk		145–148
5TWSc.07 Use a range of secondary information sources to research and select relevant evidence to answer questions.	115, Activity 1 127, Activity 1		140–141, 148–150
Analysis, evaluation and conclusions			
5TWSa.04 Suggest how an investigation could be improved and explain any proposed changes.	119, Activity 3		142–145

Science in Context	LB pages	WB pages	TG pages
5SIC.03 Use science to support points when discussing issues, situations or actions.	123 126–127		149
5SIC.05 Discuss how the use of science and technology can have positive and negative environmental effects on their local area.	123 126–127		149

These learning objectives are reproduced from the Cambridge Primary Science curriculum framework (0097) from 2020. This Cambridge International copyright material is reproduced under licence and remains the intellectual property of Cambridge Assessment International Education.

Cross-curricular links	LB pages	WB pages	TG pages
Global Perspectives® Challenge: Where does all our packaging go?	125, Let's talk 126–127, Activity 1		149 151
Global Perspectives® Challenge: What is the cost of my stuff?	125, Activity 3		149

Focus on the Earth's atmosphere

Learner's Book
pages 114–115

Workbook page 70

Worksheet 17

Unit 9 Slides 1–2
Unit 9 Flashcards
Visuals 40–41

Unit 9 Audio

Learning objectives

- **5ESp.01** Know that the Earth is surrounded by a layer of air called the atmosphere, which is a mixture of different gases (including nitrogen, carbon dioxide and oxygen).
- **5TWSc.07** Use a range of secondary information sources to research and select relevant evidence to answer questions.

Background information

The purpose of the activity on page 114 of the *Learner's Book* is to recap on their prior knowledge of Planet Earth. Learners are asked to make a 'word picture. This is a graphics activity where an image is made up of words that are, in this case, related to planet Earth. Learners begin by listing all of the words that they can think of to do with what they know about planet Earth. As with many of these kinds of activities that are aimed at eliciting prior understanding, it is important that learners work with each other. Working together means that learners share ideas, prompt each other's memories and help each other assess and check ideas that they have. Suggest to learners that they leave space on their 'word picture' so that they can add new words as they learn them throughout this unit.

Page 115 focuses on introducing learners to information about the Earth's atmosphere. This is a layer of gases surrounding planet Earth, containing approximately 78 % nitrogen and 21 % oxygen, 0.97 % argon and 0.04 % carbon dioxide, with trace amounts of other gases, and water vapour. Learners will know this mixture as air. The atmosphere is divided into layers. Working from the Earth's surface upwards they are the troposphere, stratosphere, mesosphere, thermosphere and exosphere. The atmosphere is essential to life on Earth. It acts as a blanket protecting the planet from damaging Sun's rays and contains oxygen and carbon dioxide (for photosynthesis) for life and water.

Starter activity suggestions

Show learners Unit 9 Slide 2 (boost-learning.com) and discuss the instructions for creating a word picture. Give learners time to create their list of words, sort them into importance and design and make their poster. Display the finished posters around the classroom. Give each group time to look at each one looking for words that are similar, words that they did not think of and to learn new things.

Unit 9 Slide 2 answers

Creating a word picture

Go through the instructions for making the word picture. If you have access to Stage 4 *Learner's Books*, borrow them so that learners can return to prior learning to prompt memory. Listen to their discussions of how they think this word picture has been created.

Activity notes and answers

Page 114 Make a word picture
Activity 1
Give learners time to visit each other's word pictures, bringing together their ideas and discussions relating to what they know about Planet Earth. You could scribe key ideas that emerge.

Page 115 The atmosphere
Activity 1
a 5 layers: troposphere, stratosphere, mesosphere, thermosphere and exosphere
b No. Check that learners have found at least one difference between each layer.
c Troposphere and stratosphere
d Mesosphere
e Example: Mars has a very thin atmosphere that is nearly all carbon dioxide. Saturn's atmosphere has winds that are among the fastest in the Solar System, reaching speeds of 1 800 kilometres per hour.

Activity 2
Work through the instructions step by step with the class. Learners should add the information to their booklet as mini-facts. Check that learners do not copy verbatim from the internet.

Further activities

- Give learners Worksheet 17 (boost-learning.com) to complete information about the Earth's atmosphere.
- Ask learners to complete *Workbook* page 70.

Worksheet 17 answers

1 Check that learners have written the names of the different layers, how high they are and what happens in each layer correctly.

2 Learners could share mnemonics and comment on how their mnemonic helps them to remember the different layers of the atmosphere.

Workbook answers

Page 70 The atmosphere

1 oxygen   nitrogen   carbon dioxide

2 **a** False   **b** True   **c** False   **d** True   **e** True   **f** False   **g** True

3 Example: The Earth would get hotter because the temperature would rise. It could get so hot that water would boil causing the water to disappear off the Earth and the Earth would dry out.

Assessment ideas

Use learners' word pictures as formative assessment relating to prior knowledge.

Success criteria

While completing the activities, assess and record learners.

Learning objectives	Success criteria
5ESp.01 Know that the Earth is surrounded by a layer of air called the atmosphere, which is a mixture of different gases (including nitrogen, carbon dioxide and oxygen).	Learners can describe the Earth's atmosphere.
5TWSc.07 Use a range of secondary information sources to research and select relevant evidence to answer questions.	Learners can research information about the Earth's atmosphere.

Focus on the water cycle

Learner's Book
pages 116–119

Workbook pages 71–73

Worksheet 18

Unit 9 Slide 3
Visuals 42–44

Learning objectives

- **5ESc.01** Describe the water cycle (limited to evaporation, condensation and precipitation).
- **5TWSm.01** Know that a model presents an object, process or idea in a way that shows some of the important features.
- **5TWSm.02** Use models, including diagrams, to represent and describe scientific phenomena and ideas.
- **5TWSa.04** Suggest how an investigation could be improved and explain any proposed changes.

Background information

The purpose of the activities on pages 116–119 of the Learner's Book is for learners to develop their understanding of the water cycle by applying what they have learnt about evaporation and condensation to gain an understanding of how the water cycle works. They will also consolidate their knowledge by making a model of the water cycle.

Water is everywhere on Earth. It is constantly moving, being recycled repeatedly. This process is called the 'water cycle'. Energy from the Sun drives this process. Evaporation and condensation both play an important role in the water cycle. Water from the surface of the ocean, lakes and rivers evaporates into the atmosphere. Living things also give off water vapour. When water vapour is cooled (for example, by rising to higher altitudes where the temperature is low), it condenses to form tiny water droplets. These droplets clump together to form clouds. The water from the clouds falls back to Earth as precipitation, usually in the form of rain or snow. This water eventually finds its way back into the oceans, lakes or rivers, or into living things, and the process starts again. The process is described as a cycle because it repeats itself continually.

Starter activity suggestions

- Ask learners: *Where does rain come from?* Ask learners to draw diagrams showing their understanding, and explain their diagram to a partner. In their explanation, challenge learners to use the words 'evaporate/evaporation' and 'condense/condensation'.
- Ask one or more learners to explain their thinking to the class. Do not correct misconceptions; use this opportunity as a formative assessment to see where learners' ideas are at this point.
- Show learners Unit 9 Slide 3 (boost-learning.com).

Unit 9 Slide 3 answers

The water cycle

a Accept reasonable answers and reasons.

b Condensation is the change from a vapour to a liquid. Evaporation is the change of a liquid to a gas.

c Examples: puddles, leaves giving off water, rainfall, washing drying on a line

Activity notes and answers

Page 116 Water on Earth
Let's talk
a Examples: washing, cleaning the car, cooking
b Examples: reservoir, river, water treatment works, well
c Listen to learners sharing ideas. Which ideas are secure and which do you need to go over with learners?

Let's talk

Safe water, sanitation and hygienic conditions were essential during the Covid-19 outbreak. People needed to prevent the spread of Covid-19 through contaminated hands, surfaces, and so on, so clean water was essential. Check that learners understand how infections can be spread and why washing and cleaning is important.

Let's talk

a Examples: not being able to keep clean, not being able to wash clothes, drink clean water

b Listen to learners sharing ideas. How well do they understand the impact of not having access to clean water?

Let's talk

Goal 6: Clean water and sanitation

Pages 117 The water cycle

Let's talk

a Evaporation happens when water changes from a liquid to a gas, such as water evaporating from a puddle.

b Condensation happens when warm air meets a cold surface and changes state from a gas (water vapour) to a liquid, such as warm air in a bathroom condensing on a mirror.

Activity 1

For example: It is called the water cycle because the water keeps going round and round – evaporating, condensing, evaporating.

Page 118 Making a model of the water cycle

Activity 1

a–c Get learners to discuss the illustration, how it is set up and what it represents. If they are unsure, tell them to re-read the diagram and explanation on page 117 before they create their own model. Get learners to check their model against the illustration on page 118 and check their annotations on the photograph.

> **Work safely** ⚠
>
> Ensure that learners work safely with hot water.

d–e Check learners' explanations, ensuring that they use scientific vocabulary and explain how water in the cycle can exist as solid, liquid and gas.

f Engage the class in a discussion about the usefulness of the model in helping them to understand how the water cycle works. Ask: *Which parts of the model were useful? Which parts were not? Which did you find more useful, the diagram or the physical model? Why? How would you improve the model?*

Activity 2

Learners practise and then perform their role play. Listen to learners' feedback. Challenge them to comment on what they thought was good about the model and what they thought could be improved and why.

Page 119 Which model of the water cycle is best?

Activity 1

a Example: Water was placed in the plastic bag and put somewhere warm. The water in the plastic bag evaporated, it could not get out of the bag, so it hit the sides of the bag that were cooler. It condensed into water droplets that went back down into the water (because of gravity).

b The writing on the bag describes the water cycle so that it looks like the water in the bag is part of the water cycle, the water evaporates, condenses on the sides of the bag and goes back into the sea (water at the bottom of the bag) and evaporates and the cycle continues.

Activity 2

Accept learners' responses as long as they can justify their choice in terms of modelling the water cycle, for example, because it clearly shows the cyclical nature of the water cycle.

Activity 3

Give learners the opportunity to improve their models. For example they might include more annotations, write in a different place. Make sure they comment on why they think it is an improved model.

Further activities

- Learners could write a 'story' telling the journey of a drop of water. Allow learners to be creative in their approach to telling the story of a drop of water, but help them to ensure that the scientific principles behind the story are correct.
- Ask learners to complete *Workbook* pages 71–73.
- Give learners Worksheet 18 (boost-learning.com). Make sure that learners follow instructions correctly and measure accurately. They should report that the water in the bowl has evaporated and condensed into the mug.

Workbook answers

Page 71 Water on Earth

1 Examples: salt; soil; pollution

2 This provides an opportunity for learners to apply knowledge from Unit 5 States of matter where learners evaporated water from a salt solution to leave the salt behind. Check that learners understand the process through the explanation of their prediction.

Page 72 The water cycle

1 precipitation, condensation, evaporation, collection

2 rain, snow, sleet, hail

3 The puddle forms part of the water cycle because it will evaporate, then condense as clouds. As the water droplets get heavier, they fall as rain creating new puddles that will evaporate and the cycle continues.

4 The water I drank today came from the tap. Before that, it could have come from a reservoir. The water in the reservoir could have come from rain from the clouds. The clouds are condensed water that might have evaporated from the sea.

Page 73 Modelling the water cycle

1

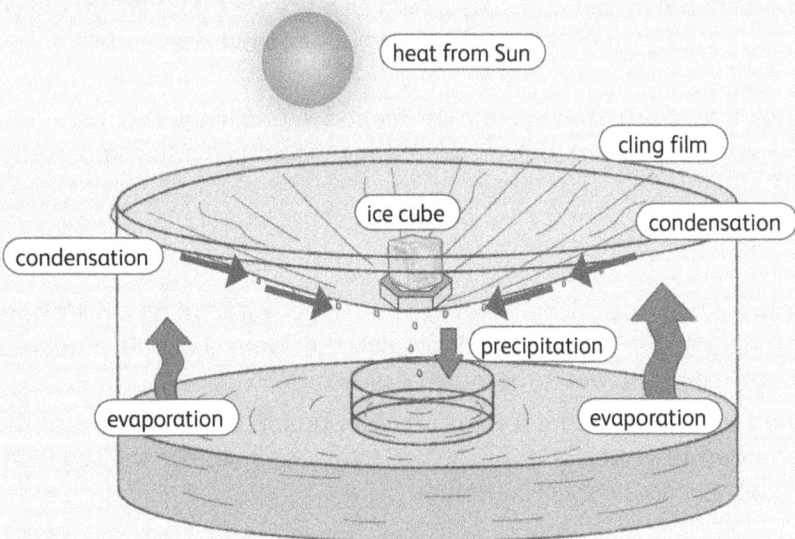

2 The water is heated by the Sun and evaporates from the bottom of the container. When the water vapour meets the colder cling film and the ice, it condenses and runs.

3 There is no known water on the Moon, therefore there is no water cycle.

ICT links

Learners photograph their model and annotate the photograph.

Assessment ideas

Use the model and role modelling as a formative assessment to find out if learners understand and can apply the water cycle to different contexts.

Success criteria

While completing the activities, assess and record learners.

Learning objectives	Success criteria
5ESc.01 Describe the water cycle (limited to evaporation, condensation and precipitation).	Learners can describe the water cycle, they explain evaporation, condensation and precipitation.
5TWSm.01 Know that a model presents an object, process or idea in a way that shows some of the important features.	Learners can discuss how a model represents the main features of the water cycle.
5TWSm.02 Use models, including diagrams, to represent and describe scientific phenomena and ideas.	Learners can discuss how a model represents the process of the water cycle.
5TWSa.04 Suggest how an investigation could be improved and explain any proposed changes.	Learners can make suggestions on how a model of the water cycle can be improved.

Focus on water pollution

Learner's Book
pages 120–122

Unit 9 Slides 4–6

Learning objectives

- **5ESp.02** Understand that most water on Earth is not pure and has dissolved substances in it.
- **5ESp.03** Understand that pollution is the introduction of substances by humans that harm the environment and identify examples of pollution.
- **5TWSc.03** Choose equipment to carry out an investigation and use it appropriately.
- **5TWSc.04** Decide when observations and measurements need to be repeated to give more reliable data.
- **5TWSp.02** Know the features of the five main types of scientific enquiry.

Background information

Pages 120–122 of the *Learner's Book* introduce ideas related to pollution and provide an opportunity for learners to investigate water pollution relating to the everyday household product, washing-up liquid. They carry out a fair test to investigate whether the advert for an eco-friendly washing-up liquid is true, that it does not pollute compared with ordinary washing-up liquid. Discuss and carry out similar tests to answer learners' own questions and prove predictions. Pollution takes many different forms and is defined as when chemicals, gases or smoke that are harmful to living things are introduced to the environment. Some forms of pollution are obvious because they are easily seen by learners such as litter, exhaust fumes from cars, smoke from factory chimneys, plastic on the beach and in seas or rubbish in streams and rivers.

Other pollution is less obvious such chemicals from household cleaners. This activity aims to help learners understand that some pollution is hard to see but can have an impact on, for example, plants in the environment.

Starter activity suggestions

- Ask learners to discuss what they think pollution is and share ideas with the rest of the class.
- Show learners Unit 9 Slides 4–6 (boost-learning.com) and discuss the different kinds of pollution.

Unit 9 Slide 4 answers

Different kinds of pollution

a and **b** At this point, learners might not know about all the kinds of pollution – do return to this slide later in the unit to reinforce learning.

1 Oil pollution in sea – can kill fish and birds.

2 Pesticides being sprayed – can kill insects that are not harmful to crops, for example pollinators.

3 Industrial chimney giving out smoke – send dangerous chemicals into the air, increase cases of asthma.

4 Polluted river – can kill fish and birds.

5 Rubbish dump – chemicals seep into the soil and waterways.

c and **d** Challenge learners to listen to each other, ask them to think about how they could convince others in the class that their suggested pollution is the worst. What reasons can they give? Encourage learners to use their own experience or knowledge to back up their reasons.

Unit 9 Slide 5 answers

Light and sound pollution

a Ask learners if they think light and sound can be a kind of pollution, if so, why and have they come across sound and light pollution? How does it affect them?

b Collect learners' ideas about how noise and light pollution affect people. They could carry out a survey in school or with friends and family at home.

c Noise and light pollution can affect animals, for example, nocturnal animals sleep during the day and are active at night; too much light can make their habitat more like day when it is night and disrupt their feeding habits. Noise pollution can affect the ultrasonic rays that bats use to locate food; noise from ships in the ocean can affect orcas' (killer whales) ability to navigate oceans.

Unit 9 Slide 6 answers

Fatberg

Collect learners' questions and ask them to find the answers as part of a home/school research activity.

Activity notes and answers

Pages 120 and 121 Water pollution (1)
Activity 1
a Washing-up liquid A: the leaves are brown and unhealthy. Washing-up liquid B: the plant is dead. Washing-up liquid C: the plant is bigger and has healthy leaves.

b Washing-up liquid B because the plant is dead.

c Washing-up liquid C: eco-friendly because the plant is healthy and green.

d Use more than one plant for each washing-up liquid. It might be that the plant used with a washing-up liquid was not a healthy plant at the beginning.

e Example: We tested eco-friendly washing-up liquid against ordinary washing-up liquid and found that the plants grew better in the eco-friendly liquid. We think that the eco-friendly is less polluting, so would be better to use.

f harmful chemicals

g The pondweed might die, the duck would have no food and could die, so the fox would not have food and would have to find something else to eat or die.

Page 122 Water pollution (2)

Let's talk

a Do washing-up liquids harm plants?

b They could test washing-up liquids on different plants.

c pondweed, containers, washing-up liquid, measuring jugs, camera

d Use more than one pondweed plant for each type of washing-up liquid (3–5 plants for each washing-up liquid).

e Fair test where they observe over time and look for patterns in the data.

f The aim of sharing ideas with the rest of the class is to learn from others so that a group might be able to improve their test before they begin.

Let's talk

a The word fatbergs is of course similar to iceberg – but made mainly of fat instead of ice. They are preventable because they form from fat, oil and grease, as well as wet wipes, disposable nappies and other items flushed down toilets.

b Accept reasonable answers.

c Many countries have problems with fatbergs, particularly in large cities. It is a growing problem but there will be some countries in the world that do not currently have this problem.

d Do not put cooking fats, oils and grease down the drain at home; do not put wet wipes or disposable nappies down the toilet.

Further activities

Learners could find out what the biggest fatberg ever discovered was. They can create a fatberg display the size of the fatberg on the school playground with information inside the fatberg itself, and leave it for other classes to view and learn from.

ICT links

Learners can use the internet to research fatbergs.

Assessment ideas

Learners could return to their planet Earth word picture and add new words relating to what they have learnt so far.

Success criteria

While completing the activities, assess and record learners.

Learning objectives	Success criteria
5ESp.02 Understand that most water on Earth is not pure and has dissolved substances in it.	Learners know that water is a solvent and has dissolved substances in it.
5ESp.03 Understand that pollution is the introduction of substances by humans that harm the environment and identify examples of pollution.	Learners can identify different kinds of pollution and explain why it is harmful to the environment.
5TWSc.03 Choose equipment to carry out an investigation and use it appropriately.	Learners can say which equipment to use to carry out an investigation.
5TWSc.04 Decide when observations and measurements need to be repeated to give more reliable data.	Learners can say how to get more reliable data.
5TWSp.02 Know the features of the five main types of scientific enquiry.	Learners can identify the scientific enquiry.

Focus on the plastics problem

Learner's Book
pages 123–125

Unit 9 Slides 7–8

Learning objectives

- **5ESp.03** Understand that pollution is the introduction of substances by humans that harm the environment and identify examples of pollution.
- **5SIC.03** Use science to support points when discussing issues, situations or actions.
- **5SIC.05** Discuss how the use of science and technology can have positive and negative environmental effects on their local area.

Background information

The activities on pages 123–125 of the *Learner's Book* focus on the issue of microbeads and microfibres, both of which contribute to plastic pollution. Microplastic beads are very small beads of plastic that do not dissolve or break down in water. Because they are so small, they pass through filters at water treatment centres and can end up in waterways and oceans. The main problem with microbeads is that they absorb toxins (poisons) that affect animals that ingest them. Countries are beginning to ban the use of microbeads. However, the problem is that they are already in the environment. Microfibres pose similar issues, when washed clothing made from synthetic materials (acrylic, polyester and nylon) shed tiny plastic fibres like microbeads. These end up in the environment and do not degrade. They also release particles into the air that can be breathed in and lead to health issues such as asthma. These pieces of plastic are ingested by animals. Animals lower down in the food chain are eaten in great quantities by larger animals, which are poisoned by the toxins in plastics.

The activities on these pages provide opportunities to debate issues relating to plastics pollution, and how science and technology have positive and negative effects on the environment.

Starter activity suggestions

Ask learners to think about the words 'microbeads' and 'microfibres', looking at the prefix 'micro' and work out what the words mean.

Activity notes and answers

Page 123 Science in context: The plastic problem: microbeads
Activity 1
Display products such as facial scrubs, toothpaste, hand soap, body wash and cosmetics that might contain microbeads. Ask learners to check the labels. Hopefully, none will be found, but if any, discuss why.

Page 124 Washing clothes and water pollution (1)
Activity 1
Learners should find that when they take out the filter paper and look at it with a magnifying glass/digital microscope, they can see evidence of microfibres. These can end up passing through waste water treatment plants into rivers and the sea.

Page 125 Washing clothes and water pollution (2)
Activity 1
a To show that there were no microfibres in the water before the fabric was washed.
b Microfibres.
c It shows that when some fabrics are washed microfibres shed off the fabric, these fibres can get into rivers and seas.

Activity 2
Learners choose different fabrics, including natural fabrics such as cotton and wool, repeating the process and recording what they see under a microscope.

Let's talk
a The plastic does not end up in a landfill or in the environment. It is recycled and made into new clothes for people, which means that new materials do not have to be made.
b Clothes made from recycled plastics when washed will release microfibres, which cause problems in the environment.
c and d Give learners time to be creative in designing their solution to this problem. Ask them to share ideas with the class. Learners could vote on which design they thought might be the best solution.

Activity 3
This activity could be carried out individually or as a group. The latter could promote interesting discussion and debate. Listen to discussions and ask learners to share their ideas.

Further activities

- Show learners Unit 9 Slides 7 and 8 (boost-learning.com) and discuss the questions raised.
- Let learners use a plastic container to make something new that is useful – reusing it rather than throwing it away.

Global Perspectives® Challenge

Where does all our packaging go?
What can we do about packaging that ends up in the ocean?

Let's talk
Ask learners to think of ways to reduce plastic and other pollution from getting into the environment and in particular the oceans.

Global Perspectives® Challenge

What is the cost of my stuff?
What resources do you 'need'?
What things do you 'want'?

Activity 3
Learners discuss their tables of wants and needs. Ask learners to think about the natural resources and raw materials used to make the objects on their lists.

Unit 9 Slide 7 answers

Messages about plastic

a Accept reasonable answers.

b Accept reasonable answers.

c Discuss issues, for example animals eating plastic, getting trapped in pieces of plastic and so on.

d Listen to their response. You could create a Plastics Pledge display, where learners can record what they can do that is achievable.

e Listen and record their responses, perhaps on the display.

Unit 9 Slide 8 answers

How you and your family can do swaps to help the environment

Accept learners' responses. They could choose from the suggestions and add ideas of their own.

ICT links

Learners could use a digital microscope to view microfibres.

Success criteria

While completing the activities, assess and record learners.

Learning objectives	Success criteria
5ESp.03 Understand that pollution is the introduction of substances by humans that harm the environment and identify examples of pollution.	Learners explain how microbeads and microfibres are pollution created by humans and how they affect the environment.
5SIC.03 Use science to support points when discussing issues, situations or actions.	Learners debate issues relating to pollution and consider their own actions.
5SIC.05 Discuss how the use of science and technology can have positive and negative environmental effects on their local area.	Learners discuss how technology, for example making materials such as plastics and fabrics affect the environment.

Focus on other kinds of pollution

Learner's Book
pages 126–128

Workbook pages 74–75

Worksheet 19

Unit 9 Flashcards

Unit 9 Audio

Learning objectives

- **5ESp.03** Understand that pollution is the introduction of substances by humans that harm the environment and identify examples of pollution.
- **5TWSc.07** Use a range of secondary information sources to research and select relevant evidence to answer questions.
- **5SIC.03** Use science to support points when discussing issues, situations or actions.
- **5SIC.05** Discuss how the use of science and technology can have positive and negative environmental effects on their local area.

Background information

The aim of pages 126 and 127 of the *Learner's Book* is to show learners different kinds of pollution, some that they might already know about. For each example, the text provides information on the positive and negative viewpoints relating to each one. While pollution is a serious issue, learners should also be offered an alternative viewpoint, since many of the pollutants are important to communities, for example oil for heating, factories for making goods, and so on. The issue is what do we use, how we use it and how we can we reduce pollution. Page 127 focuses on learners developing their skills in researching information on pollution and developing their ability to communicate to an audience what they have found out.

Starter activity suggestions

- Ask learners to list all the different kinds of pollution that they know about.
- Ask learners to think about where they have seen or experienced pollution. Ask: *What was it like? How did it make you feel? Where do they think local pollution comes from?*

Activity notes and answers

Pages 126 and 127 Science in context: The positive and negative effects of science
Activity 1
Give learners time to research their information. If learners are working in groups, each group could research one aspect. Encourage them to ask questions prior to their research and use research approaches, such as note taking to support their work. Both of these approaches help to avoid learners copying verbatim from books or the internet. You could also offer online video clips for learners to watch and take notes.

Activity 2
Groups could communicate their research using a PowerPoint slide, an infographic, podcast, short film, poster or role play. If learners are unsure of an approach, for example an infographic

> **Global Perspectives® Challenge**
> **Where does all our packaging go?**
> What is ocean trash?
>
> **Activity 1**
> Have a class discussion about the types of waste that is accumulating in the oceans and how and why there is so much waste ending up in the oceans.

or podcast, suggest that they research how to create one. Encourage groups to choose their own way so that there is variety across the class. Each of these approaches is more likely to motivate learners to think about what their audience needs to know. These approaches challenge them to think more carefully about the information that they have gathered and how to present it.

Page 128 What have you learnt about Planet Earth?
Let's talk
Listen to learners' individual responses, encouraging them to use correct scientific language.

Activity 1
a Example: oil, agricultural (such as fertilisers, pesticides), air pollution, water pollution.
b Accept reasonable responses depending on the answer to **a**.

Activity 2
Check learners' diagrams.

Activity 3
Check learners' word pictures.

Further activities

- Give learners Worksheet 19 (boost-learning.com), which supports them in creating an infographic.
- Learners share or display their research. Encourage learners to interact with the information by getting groups to create questionnaires to use to learn new information from each other's work.
- Ask learners to complete *Workbook* page 74.

✐ **Workbook answers**

Page 74 Pollution

1 Check learners' mind maps.

ICT links

Learners use computers to create PowerPoints, infographics, posters, podcasts, and so on.

Assessment ideas

- Use the Flashcards and Audio recordings (boost-learning.com) to assess that learners know and understand the new words and concepts covered in this unit.
- Ask learners to complete the checklist on page 128 of the *Learner's Book*, and the self-check activity on page 75 of the *Workbook*.

Success criteria

While completing the activities, assess and record learners.

Learning objectives	Success criteria
5ESp.03 Understand that pollution is the introduction of substances by humans that harm the environment and identify examples of pollution.	Learners explain the different kinds of pollution and their effects.
5TWSc.07 Use a range of secondary information sources to research and select relevant evidence to answer questions.	Learners research information different kinds of pollution.
5SIC.03 Use science to support points when discussing issues, situations or actions.	Learners debate issues relating to pollution and consider their own actions.
5SIC.05 Discuss how the use of science and technology can have positive and negative environmental effects on their local area.	Learners discuss how science and technology can affect the environment.

Unit 10 The Earth in space

Learning objectives from Stages 1–4	LB pages	WB pages	TG pages
4ESs.01 *Explain why the spinning of the Earth on its axis leads to the apparent movement of the Sun, night and day, and changes in shadows.*	129–130	76	154–155

Learning objectives overview

Earth and Space	Online resources	LB pages	WB pages	TG pages
Earth in space	Flashcards/Audio			
5ESs.01 Describe the orbit of the Earth around the Sun (limited to slight ellipse, anticlockwise direction and the duration).	Unit 10 Slide 3	131–133		156–157
5ESs.02 Describe how the tilt of the Earth can create different seasons in different places.	Unit 10 Slide 4	134–137	77	157–159
5ESs.03 Know that a satellite is an object in space that orbits a larger object and a moon is a natural satellite that orbits a planet.		138–140	78	160–162

Thinking and Working Scientifically	LB pages	WB pages	TG pages
Models and representations			
5TWSm.02 Use models, including diagrams, to represent and describe scientific phenomena and ideas.	130, Activity 1-2 131, Let's talk		154–155, 156–157
Purpose and planning			
5TWSp.01 Ask scientific questions and select appropriate scientific enquiries to use.	133, Activity 1		156–157

Science in Context	LB pages	WB pages	TG pages
5SIC.03 Use science to support points when discussing issues, situations or actions.	139		161
5SIC.05 Discuss how the use of science and technology can have positive and negative environmental effects on their local area.	139		161

These learning objectives are reproduced from the Cambridge Primary Science curriculum framework (0097) from 2020. This Cambridge International copyright material is reproduced under licence and remains the intellectual property of Cambridge Assessment International Education.

Cross-curricular links	LB pages	WB pages	TG pages
Mathematics	137, Activity 1		159
English	129, Activity 1 138, Activity 1		154 160

Focus on the tilt of the Earth

Learner's Book pages 129–130

Workbook page 76

Unit 10 Slides 1–2
Unit 10 Flashcards
Visual 45

Unit 10 Audio

Learning objectives

Revision of:

- **4ESs.01** *Explain why the spinning of the Earth on its axis leads to the apparent movement of the Sun, night and day, and changes in shadows.*
- **5TWSm.02** Use models, including diagrams, to represent and describe scientific phenomena and ideas.

Background information

The purpose of page 129 of the *Learner's Book* is to revisit learning from previous stages using a KWL grid (*KWL* stands for *What I know, What I want to know, What I have learnt*). It is usually more successful when learners are asked questions that help to scaffold their thinking, as do the suggestions on page 129. Keep returning to the grid with learners so that they can add new knowledge and answers to their questions as they progress through this unit. Their personal questions could be answered as part of a home/school activity.

On page 130, learners are reminded that the Earth spins on its axis, which is tilted at an angle. This revision of knowledge is important for later in the unit when seasons are the focus of learning.

Starter activity suggestions

- Learners work through their KWL grids either as individuals or as small groups, recording on large sheets of paper, which could be displayed and added to on a regular basis.
- Show learners Unit 10 Slide 2 (boost-learning.com) to help prompt learners' memories about Earth in space.
- Use the quiz on page 76 of the *Workbook*. Learners could peer-assess because the answers are at the bottom of the page. This can be used as a formative assessment opportunity to check if there are common questions that learners answer incorrectly.

Unit 10 Slide 2 answers

What do you remember?

1 The Solar System

2 The apparent movement of the Sun

3 Day and night

4 Comets and stars, planets, asteroids, comets

Activity notes and answers

Page 129 The Earth and beyond
Activity 1
The use of question stems creates cross-curricular links with English and ESL.

a Show learners Unit 10 Slide 2 (boost-learning.com) to prompt learners' memory about past learning.

b The focus here is on seasons and satellites, narrowing down the areas that learners could ask about. This is often more effective than learners being offered an area so vast that it is harder to think of questions to ask.

c Learners carry this out, possibly as a home/school activity across the course of this topic.

d Keep returning to the grid so that learners can add to it. If the column inhibits responses, allow them to use a normal page.

Page 130 Tilt of the Earth
Activity 1
Check that the model is correct.

Activity 2
Check that in their video clip learners have the Earth and Sun (torch) in the correct position and explain the area in light as day and the area in darkness as night.

Let's talk

a Example: The people did not have scientific knowledge at that time to help them understand night and day, so they used stories.

b Copernicus put forward the theory that the Sun rather than Earth was at the centre of the universe.

Further activities

Show or give learners access to a video clip of day and night to make sure that they master this key idea if they are uncertain from previous learning.

ICT links

Learners can access video clips of day and night.

Assessment ideas

Use these pages to check how secure previous learning is and provide additional support where appropriate.

Workbook answers

Page 76 How many did you get right?

1 c	2 c	3 d	4 a

5 a False	b False	c False	d True

6 a True	b False	c False

7 a False	b True

Success criteria

While completing the activities, assess and record learners.

Learning objectives	Success criteria
4ESs.01 Explain why the spinning of the Earth on its axis leads to the apparent movement of the Sun, night and day, and changes in shadows.	Learners can explain the apparent movement of the Sun, night and day and shadows.
5TWSm.02 Use models, including diagrams, to represent and describe scientific phenomena and ideas.	Learners can understand that a model presents how the Earth is tilted and that it can show night and day.

Focus on Earth's orbit around the Sun

Learner's Book
pages 131–133

Worksheet 20

Unit 10 Slide 3

Learning objectives

- **5ESs.01** Describe the orbit of the Earth around the Sun (limited to slight ellipse, anticlockwise direction and the duration).
- **5TWSm.02** Use models, including diagrams, to represent and describe scientific phenomena and ideas.
- **5TWSp.01** Ask scientific questions and select appropriate scientific enquiries to use.

Background information

The focus of pages 131 and 132 of the *Learner's Book* is the way in which the Earth and Moon orbit the Sun. There are several key areas of learning, firstly that the Earth completes one rotation on its axis once every 24 hours. It is this movement that gives us day and night. The second key area of learning is that the Earth orbits the Sun (while it rotates on its axis once every 24 hours). This orbit is elliptical and takes a year to complete. These are challenging concepts because they are abstract. It is therefore useful, whenever possible, to get learners to model these phenomena, to get a physical feel for what happens. Discuss the importance of using models and how they can help us understand things that we cannot see happening.

Starter activity suggestions

Show learners Unit 10 Slide 3 (boost-learning.com) and use it to help learners model how the Earth rotates once every 24 hours, the Moon orbits the Earth and both orbit the Sun in an elliptical path.

Unit 10 Slide 3 answers

The Earth and Moon orbiting the Sun

Check that learners' models show:

- the Earth spinning on its axis once every 24 hours.
- the Moon orbiting the Earth
- the Earth and Moon orbiting the Sun in an elliptical path.

Ask learners to explain their model and to indicate which aspects their model has helped them to understand or remember. Learners could peer assess, commenting on each other's models.

Activity notes and answers

Page 131 Modelling the movement of the Earth and Moon around the Sun
Let's talk
Encourage groups to share their discussions on what makes a good model, for example easy to understand, clear, can be applied easily, scientifically correct, interesting. Check that learners are able to apply their criteria to each model using reasoning.

Page 132 Shape of the Earth's orbit around the Sun
Let's talk
a Their descriptions should show an understanding that the orbit is not completely round.
b The shape is an ellipse.
Activity 1
The aim of this activity is to help embed the way in which the Earth and Moon orbit the Sun. Learners should peer assess each other's diagrams.

Page 133 Elliptical path of the Earth around the Sun
Activity 1
Check learners' grids. Ask how confident they are in the ideas that they have learnt and if there is anything that they are still unsure of. They should add their information from the home/school activity and research answers to their own questions.

Activity 2
Art and science go hand in hand. Offer contexts to explore and develop artistic creativity in science. Display and celebrate learners' art.

Further activities

Give learners Worksheet 20 (boost-learning.com) to complete to ensure knowledge is embedded.

ICT links

- Learners use the internet to research answers to their questions.
- Learners could use a software program to create patterns based on ellipses.

Assessment ideas

Use learners' models and diagrams to check how secure their understanding is.

Success criteria

While completing the activities, assess and record learners.

Learning objectives	Success criteria
5ESs.01 Describe the orbit of the Earth around the Sun (limited to slight ellipse, anticlockwise direction and the duration).	Learners can describe the orbit of the Earth around the Sun.
5TWSm.02 Use models, including diagrams, to represent and describe scientific phenomena and ideas.	Learners can model the orbit of the Earth around the Sun.
5TWSp.01 Ask scientific questions and select appropriate scientific enquiries to use.	Learners can ask and research answers to their own questions.

Focus on understanding seasons

Learner's Book
pages 134–137

Workbook page 77

Unit 10 Slide 4
Visuals 46–48

Learning objectives

- **5ESs.02** Describe how the tilt of the Earth can create different seasons in different places.
- **5TWSm.02** Use models, including diagrams, to represent and describe scientific phenomena and ideas.

Background information

The aim of the activities on pages 134 and 136 of the *Learner's Book* is to develop learners' understanding about the seasons. Learners know that the Earth orbits the Sun and that the Earth spins on its axis, which is tilted. As the Earth orbits the Sun, the amount of sunlight each place on Earth receives every day changes slightly. It is this change that results in the seasons. When the North Pole tilts toward the Sun, it is summer in the northern hemisphere; when the South Pole tilts toward the Sun, it is winter in the northern hemisphere. In spring, the temperature and day length become longer and the opposite happens in autumn. There are no seasons at the equator because the Sun strikes this part of the Earth at about the same angle every day.

Page 136 poses a challenging question to learners to find out if they can apply their learning about the relationship between the Sun and the Earth; this helps to show how secure learning is about seasons. Note that the diagram on page 134 of the *Learner's Book* shows seasons from a northern hemisphere perspective.

Starter activity suggestions

Show learners Unit 10 Slide 4 (boost-learning.com) as part of the starter activity discussions.

Unit 10 Slide 4 answers

The moving Earth

a Listen to and check learners' descriptions, asking questions to formatively assess how secure their ideas are.

b–c If the Earth was tilted at 90° the North Pole would be facing straight onto the Sun resulting in 6 months of daylight and extremely high temperatures that would melt the ice cap and change the environment dramatically. Humans would not be able to live in this area. The other side of the planet would be in darkness for 6 months.

Activity notes and answers

Page 134 Understanding the seasons (1)
Activity 1
Check that learners are following the instructions correctly so that their answer is that the country; for example Canada, will face the Sun at some points and then face away at other points in the orbit.

Pages 135 and 136 Understanding the seasons (2)
Activity 1
The aim of this activity is to model what it is like when the Sun (torch) is directly overhead. The sunlight is more concentrated and the temperature hot.

Activity 2
The aim of this activity is to model what it is like when the Sun's rays strike the Earth at an angle. Learners should note that the light is spread out and is not as bright, suggesting it is not as intense and hot. The Sun's energy is less strong than in Activity 1 when the Sun was directly overhead.

Activity 3
Learners apply what they have learnt from Activities 1 and 2 to model how the Sun shines on the Earth (a globe/beach ball) at 23.5°. The temperature will be hot.

Activity 4
The light is at an angle, spread out on the southern hemisphere. It will not be as hot, so it will be winter in the southern hemisphere (summer in the northern hemisphere).

Page 137 Science in context: Seasons around the world
Let's talk
The aim is to see if learners agree which months belong to which season and to find out if they agree with the meteorological definitions of seasons.

Activity 1

This activity creates cross-curricular links with time in Mathematics.

Autumn (Fall) runs from 1 March to 31 May

Winter runs from 1 June to 31 August

Spring runs from 1 September to 30 November

Summer runs from 1 December to 28 February (29 February in a leap year).

Activity 2

Example answers:

Rainy seasons – Brazil, Southern China, India, Taiwan.

Dry seasons – Australia, African countries.

Activity 3

a–e Listen to learners' discussions, describing that permanent winter would mean very low temperatures, ice, snow, long nights and short days, farmers would find it hard to grow plants and lives would dramatically change. For example, effect of little daylight, less food available, farmers would not be able to plant crops outside, some plants and animals would become extinct.

f Give learners time to organise their ideas and script their podcast and consider, what makes a good podcast (understanding the needs of the audience, which are the most important ideas, making sure content is correct, not to overload the audience).

Further activities

- Learners work in pairs. One names a country in the world and the other has to say what season it is there at the moment and how they know.
- Ask learners to complete *Workbook* page 77.

Workbook answers

Page 77 Seasons on Earth

1 elliptical

2 a 2 – summer   b 4 – winter   c 1 – spring   d 3 – autumn

3 Because the Sun strikes the Earth at the equator at the same angle every day.

4 The seasons would reverse.

ICT links

- Learners use the internet for research.
- Learners create a podcast.

Success criteria

While completing the activities, assess and record learners.

Learning objectives	Success criteria
5ESs.02 Describe how the tilt of the Earth can create different seasons in different places.	Learners can describe how the tilt of the Earth creates seasons in different parts of the world.
5TWSm.02 Use models, including diagrams, to represent and describe scientific phenomena and ideas	Learners can explain how using models helps them to understand some things in science, for example seasons.

Focus on satellites

Learner's Book
pages 138–140

Workbook pages 78–80

Worksheet 21

Unit 10 Slides 5–7
Unit 10 Flashcards

Unit 10 Audio

Learning objectives

- **5ESs.03** Know that a satellite is an object in space that orbits a larger object and a Moon is a natural satellite that orbits a planet.
- **5SIC.03** Use science to support points when discussing issues, situations or actions.
- **5SIC.05** Discuss how the use of science and technology can have positive and negative environmental effects on their local area.

Background information

The aim of pages 138 and 139 of the *Learner's Book* is to develop learners' understanding of natural and artificial satellites. A satellite is an object that orbits a planet; the Moon is the Earth's natural satellite. There are thousands of artificial satellites, the first of which was Sputnik 1 launched in 1957. Artificial satellites have a range of functions, from photographing the Earth and deep space to supporting communication and forecasting weather. Learners can 'spot' the International Space Station (ISS) that orbits the Earth roughly every 90 minutes. Satellites use solar cells to power themselves and store energy in batteries for when they enter shadow.

As on Earth humans have created litter, items that have been discarded, in this case old satellites and parts of rockets have been left in orbit around the Earth. This is an instance of science having a negative effect on an environment (there is even debris from human activity on the Moon). As working satellites orbit the Earth, they have to avoid colliding with small pieces of debris that could damage each one. In 2006, a piece of space junk hit the ISS taking a chip out of one of the windows. Scientists are working to find ways to reduce and remove space junk, a problem caused by humans.

Starter activity suggestions

- Show learners Unit 10 Slide 5 (boost-learning.com) on the International Space Station. Check the website for when the ISS will pass over your locality so that learners can watch out for and spot the ISS.
- Show learners Unit 10 Slide 6 (boost-learning.com).
- Give learners Worksheet 21 (boost-learning.com) so that they can use it to generate questions using a range of question stems and research answers. Next to the questions, there is limited room for answers to encourage learners to precis information, not copy verbatim.

Unit 10 Slide 5 answers

Use Unit 10 Slide 5 to encourage learners to access the web to check out when they can spot the ISS moving across the night sky in their locality.

Activity notes and answers

Page 138 Satellites

Activity 1

The use of question stems creates cross-curricular links with English and ESL. Give learners time to check their KWL grids and organise what they have to do next to complete this activity.

Activity 2

Learners choose a way to communicate their research and share it with the rest of the class once completed.

Page 139 Science in context: Space junk
Activity 1
Check that learners use their research on space junk and consider the issue of audience in terms of content and how to communicate their design in an interesting way. Encourage 'blue skies' thinking, bringing creativity to this task will be important. The class should read each poster and then vote on the design that they think will be best to rid space of junk left by humans.

Further activities

- Learners research and create a timeline of the history of satellites.
- Learners complete *Workbook* pages 78 and 79.

Workbook answers

Page 78 Satellites

1 Natural satellites are not made by humans; artificial satellites are.

2 helping car Sat Navs to work
helping to predict the weather
photographing the Earth
tracking storms
tracking pollution

3 1950s

4 There are more and more being sent up to space so space is becoming cluttered. Humans leave bits of equipment and old satellites that no longer work in space. This becomes a hazard because they can crash into working satellites, the ISS and rockets, causing damage.

5 Collect and share learners' ideas.

Page 79 Space junk
Learners can use this page to plan their poster (page 135 in the *Learner's Book*).

ICT links

- Learners use the internet for research.
- Learners use an app for locating the ISS.

Assessment ideas

- Use the Flashcards and Audio recordings (boost-learning.com) to assess that learners know and understand the new words and concepts covered in this unit.
- Ask learners to complete the checklist on page 140 of the *Learner's Book*, and the self-check activity on page 80 of the *Workbook*.

Success criteria

While completing the activities, assess and record learners.

Learning objectives	Success criteria
5ESs.03 Know that a satellite is an object in space that orbits a larger object and a moon is a natural satellite that orbits a planet.	Learners can explain the difference between an artificial and natural satellite.
5SIC.03 Use science to support points when discussing issues, situations or actions.	Learners can discuss issues linked to 'Space Junk'.
5SIC.05 Discuss how the use of science and technology can have positive and negative environmental effects on their local area.	Learners can explain why 'Space Junk' has a negative effect on their local space environment.

Scientific dictionary

A

Adapt When a plant or an animal changes to suit its environment

Adaptation When a plant or an animal is suited to where it lives

Air particles Tiny particles of the gas air, which we cannot see

Air resistance Friction between a moving object and the surrounding air

Anomalous Something that does not fit the pattern

Anther Part of a flower; the part of the stamen that makes and stores pollen

Anticlockwise Turning in the opposite direction to the hands of a clock moving round

Applied force A force that is applied (used) on an object by a person or another object

Artificial satellites Satellites that are built by humans and orbit the Earth; for example communication satellites, weather satellites and the International Space Station

Atmosphere The layer of air surrounding the Earth

B

Behaves The way a human or other animal acts

Boiling When a material, such as water, changes from liquid to a gas

Boiling point The point at which a liquid boils; the boiling point of water is 100 °C

Botanist A scientist who studies plants

C

Camouflage Colours or patterns on an animal's body that help to hide it from predators or prey

Carbohydrates Also called starches; they include bread, crackers, noodles, pasta and rice

Carbon dioxide A colourless and odourless gas

Carpel The female part of a flower

Classification key Something that helps you identify what something, like a plant or an animal, is; also known as an identification key

Column of air For example, the air inside a tube

Concentration The strength of a solution; how much is dissolved in a solution

Condensation The process in which a gas changes state into a liquid; for example, when water vapour condenses to become water

Condenses When something changes from a gas into a liquid, specifically when it cools

D

Dairy foods A type of food produced from, or containing, the milk of mammals such as sheep, cows, goats, camels and buffalo

Data Information (often in the form of numbers)

Digestion The process of digesting food

Digestive system The parts of the body that work together to extract the nutrients and energy the body needs from the food you eat

Dispersal Spreading something, for example seeds, from one place to another

Dissect Cut something up

Dissolve A solid that mixes in a liquid until it cannot be seen

E

Eco-friendly Not harmful to the environment

Ellipse An oval shape

Embryo The part of the seed that grows into a plant

Evaporates When something changes from a liquid into a gas when it heats up

Evaporation The process in which a liquid changes state into a gas; for example, when water evaporates to become water vapour

Excrete To get rid of waste from the body

Extinct A group of living things that have died out altogether (such as a dodo)

Extract To remove or take something out

F

Faeces The solid waste humans and other animals get rid of from their bodies by passing it through the anus

Fertilisation The process in which a male cell from a grain of pollen combines with a female cell in a flower's ovule; fertilisation must take place before a fruit grows and seeds form

Filament Part of a flower; the part of the stamen that holds up the anther

Flowering plants Plants that produce flowers

Force diagram A diagram that uses arrows to show the size and direction of forces acting on objects

Force field The area around a magnet where a magnetic force can be detected

Freezing When a liquid turns into a solid

Fresh water Water from lakes, rivers, snow and ice which is not salty; water that people can drink

Friction The force created when an object moves across the surface of another object; friction always acts in the opposite direction to the direction of movement

G

Gas One of the three states of matter; substance that has no fixed shape or volume and spreads out to fill any container; most gases are invisible

Germinated Begun to grow

Germination rates The percentage of seeds that germinate out of the total number of seeds planted; for example, if 100 tomato seeds are planted and 75 of them germinate, the germination rate is 75 %

Gliders Seeds that have wings to help them disperse

Gravity The force that keeps the planets in motion around the Sun and causes objects near the Earth to fall towards it

H

Hydrogen A gas that is colourless and does not smell

I

Identification key Something that helps you identify what something, like a plant or an animal, is; also known as a classification key

Insoluble Does not dissolve in a liquid

Invisible Cannot be seen

Iron filings Very small pieces of iron used to show the direction of a magnetic field

L

Large intestine A tube that is part of the digestive system that goes from the lower end of your stomach to your anus

Life cycle The series of stages in the growth of a living thing

Line graph A type of graph where the data is marked in dots (a series of points) joined by straight lines

M

Magnetic field The area around a magnet that is affected by the magnetic force of a magnet

Melting The process in which a solid changes state to become a liquid; for example, ice changing to water when heated

Microbeads Very small pieces of plastic

Microfibres Very small fibres from fabric

Microplastic Tiny pieces of plastic that are often too small to be seen without a microscope

N

Natural satellites Objects that orbit (go around) a planet; known as moons

Nectar Sugary liquid produced by flowers to attract pollinators like insects

Nitrogen A colourless gas that does not smell and makes up about 78 % of the air that we breathe

Non-flowering plant A plant that does not produce flowers

Non-standard measurements Measurements that are not usually used, such as a pencil, an arm or a shoe

Normal force The force that the ground (or any surface) pushes back up with

Nutrients Substances found in the soil that plants need to grow and be healthy

O

Oesophagus The tube that links the mouth to the stomach

Orbit The path that an object takes in space when it goes around a star or a planet

Ovary Part of a flower; the part of the carpel that becomes the fruit after fertilisation

Ovules Parts of a flower; the parts inside the ovary that become the seeds after fertilisation

P

Percussion instrument Musical instrument that make sounds when you hit or shake them

Pitch How high or low a sound is

Pollen A fine powder on the male part of the flower; pollen contains the male cell needed for reproduction

Pollinated When pollen from the male part of the plant, the anther, has been moved to the female part of the plant, the stigma, to fertilise the plant

Pollination The process of moving pollen from the male part of the plant, the anther, to the female part of the plant, the stigma, to fertilise the plant

Pollinators Animals that move pollen from the male part of the plant, the anther, to the female part of the plant, the stigma

Pollution Something that is introduced into the environment that is dirty, unclean or is harmful; such as car exhaust fumes, litter, oil spills

Polyester A fabric that is made from a type of plastic

Precipitation Rain, sleet, snow or hail

Predator An animal that hunts and kills other animals for food

Predator adaptations The characteristics that predators have to help them catch their prey; for example, eagles have large talons

Prey Animals that are hunted, killed and eaten by predators

Prey adaptations An adaptation that helps an animal to avoid being eaten

Protein A nutrient found in food such as meat, milk, eggs, and beans

R

Reaction force An upward force that acts against weight

Reproduce When living things make copies of themselves; for example, animals have young, plants make new plants

Reproduction (in plants) When a male cell from one plant combines with a female cell of another plant to make seeds that grow into new plants

Retractable claws Claws that can be moved back into the paws when not in use

Reversible A change that can be undone; can be reversed, changed back

S

Saliva A watery fluid that moistens food and starts to break it down before it goes down the oesophagus to the stomach

Satellites Objects that orbit a planet; can be natural or artificial

Scented Has a smell

Seasons The four different times of the year with different types of weather; the seasons are spring, summer, autumn (fall) and winter

Seed coat The outside covering on a seed

Shakers A type of seed container, like a pepper pot, that disperses seeds when it is shaken by the wind

Small intestine Where most digestion takes place and where nutrients from the broken-down food get absorbed into the body

Soluble Dissolves in a liquid

Solute In a solution, the solid you dissolve into a liquid; for example, sugar is the solute when it is dissolved in water

Solution A mixture of a solid and a liquid that looks clear and has no particles floating in it

Solvent In a solution, the liquid into which a solid has dissolved; for example, water is the solvent when sugar is dissolved in water

Space junk Disused satellites and other man-made debris in orbit around the Earth

Stamen The male part of a flower

Standard measurements Measurements used to measure mass, length, capacity and temperature; the same measurements are used across the world

Stigma Part of a flower; the part of the carpel that receives pollen

Stomach The internal organ where food is broken down; part of the digestive system

Streamlined Something that is designed to reduce air or water resistance

String instrument Musical instrument, like a guitar, played by plucking or stroking strings with the fingers or with a bow

Style Part of a flower; the part of the carpel that received pollen

Suspension A mixture of materials in which a solid is mixed with a liquid but has not yet dissolved; you can see particles floating in a suspension

T

Temperature A measure of how hot something is, measured in °C

U

Upthrust The upward force of water

V

Vibrate When something moves back and forwards, from side to side, or up and down very quickly

Vibrating When something is moving backwards and forwards, from side to side, or up and down very quickly

Vibration When you can feel something moving backwards and forwards, from side to side, or up and down very quickly

Volume The loudness of a sound

W

Water cycle The process in which the water on Earth is continually moving around, through repeated evaporation and condensation

Water resistance Friction between a moving object and the surrounding water

Water vapour Water in the form of gas

Wind instruments Musical instruments, like a flute, in which sound is produced by the vibration of air, usually by blowing into the instrument